S0-ADL-018

FIRST CONTACT

DR. CORNELIUS J. JAENEN

CANADA
A PEOPLE'S HISTORY

Fitzhenry & Whiteside

National Library of Canada Cataloguing in Publication

Jaenen, Cornelius J., 1927-
    First contact / Cornelius Jaenen.

(Canada: a people's history)
Includes bibliographical references and index.
ISBN 1-55041-443-7

1. Indians of North America—First contact with Europeans—Canada—Juvenile literature. 2. Canada—History—To 1663 (New France)—Juvenile literature. 3. Native peoples—Canada—History—Juvenile literature. I. Title. II. Series: Canada : a people's history (Markham, Ont.)

E78.C2J33 2005   j971.01   C2005-900967-2

All inquiries should be addressed to: In the United States:
Fitzhenry & Whiteside Limited   121 Harvard Avenue, Suite 2
195 Allstate Parkway   Allston, Massachusetts 02134
Markham, Ontario L3R 4T8

www.fitzhenry.ca   godwit@fitzhenry.ca

Fitzhenry & Whiteside acknowledges with thanks the Canada Council for the Arts, the Government of Canada through its Book Publishing Industry Development Program, and the Ontario Arts Council for their support in our publishing program.

Fitzhenry & Whiteside is grateful to the Canadian Broadcasting Corporation for its assistance in the preparation of this volume in the book series based on its 17-episode, bilingual television documentary series, *Canada: A People's History*. For more information about *Canada: A People's History*, please visit **www.cbc.ca/history**.
Canada: A People's History © 2000, 2001 Canadian Broadcasting Corporation

Book Credits
Series Consultant: Donald Bogle
Project Manager: Doug Panasis / www.Resources.too
Senior Editor: Loralee Case
Photo Researcher: Lisa Brant
Editorial Coordinator: Amy Hingston
Copy Editor/Indexer: Penny Hozy
Layout and Designer: Fortunato Design Inc.

Canadian Broadcasting Corporation Credits:
CBC Representative: Karen Bower

Printed and bound in Canada.
1 2 3 4 5   08 07 06 05 04

Contents

INTRODUCTION   1
  The Big Idea   1
  Picture This   2
  Setting the Scene   4

CHAPTER 1   THE FIRST PEOPLES   7
  Since Time Began   8
  Many People, Many Languages   10
  Aboriginal Spiritual Beliefs   11
  Aboriginal Government   12
  Government in the Iroquois Confederacy   13
  Who Owned the Land?   14
  The Root of All Evil   14
  Trade Relations   15
  On the Eve of Contact   15

CHAPTER 2   EARLY EXPLORERS AND SETTLERS   17
  The Quest for Wealth and Power   18
  Columbus Believes the Earth Is Round   18
  Cabot Claims a "New Founde Land"   19
  Cartier Makes Contact   20
  Disaster at Ste. Croix   24
  The Order of Good Cheer   25
  Champlain Builds a Fortress   26

CHAPTER 3   ECONOMIC CONTACT   29
  "Sea Silver"—The Bounty of the Cod Fishery   30
  Preserving the Catch   31
  The Tragedy of the Beothuk   32
  The Ancient Pursuit of Whaling   34
  The Whale Hunt   35
  Whaling in the Arctic   36
  Whaling Effects the Inuit   36
  The Fur Trade Begins   37
  The Fur Trade Expands   38

The Coureurs de Bois   38
Étienne Brûlé   39
Military Alliances Secure the Fur Trade   40
A Costly Alliance   41
Death of a Nation   41
The Voyageurs Travel Deeper into the Continent   42
The Impact of the Fur Trade on Aboriginal Peoples   43

Chapter 4 An Age of Faith   45

Spreading Christianity Around the World   46
Two Different World Views   46
The Missionaries Come to New France   47
The Huron Carol   49
Religious Women of New France   50
Kateri Tekakwitha: Lily of the Mohawks   52
Death, Fear, and Resentment   53
Sainte-Marie-among-the-Hurons   54
A Nation D.estroyed   55

Chapter 5 Fast Forward   57

Losing Their Rights   58
Settling Land Claims   58
The Richest Claim of All   60
The Debate Over Self-Government   61
Toward a Better Future   61
Aboriginal Peoples in Canada Today   62

Glossary   65
Index   66
Credits   67

Cultural Areas
- Arctic
- Subarctic
- Western Plateau
- West Coast
- Great Plains
- Northeastern Woodlands

THE BIG IDEA

Aboriginal peoples had lived across North America for thousands of years. They had practiced a **world view** in which everyone shared the land and its resources. They viewed nature's resources as gifts, and they used these gifts wisely. They made sure that nature's resources would still be there for their children and their grandchildren to use.

Then, around 1600, Europeans came to North America. Their world view was very different from that of Aboriginal peoples. To the Europeans, land was not something people shared. It was something people owned. The Europeans were interested in what they could gain from the land and its resources. This set the stage for a collision course between two different sets of values.

When Europeans came to North America, they gave names to the different Aboriginal groups they met, such as the Huron and the Iroquois. Until recently, these names were commonly used. Today, though, many Aboriginal groups prefer to use the names they have always called themselves, such as the Wendat (Huron) and the Haudenosaunee (Iroquois). These are the names that appear on this map. Why do you think this is important to Aboriginal peoples?

TIMELINE

1000 CE Norse Vikings make the earliest-known European contact with Aboriginal peoples at L'Anse aux Meadows, Newfoundland.

1497 John Cabot arrives in North America somewhere along the North Atlantic coast.

1535 On his second voyage, Cartier travels the St. Lawrence River as far as Hochelaga (present-day Montreal).

1550 Cod from the North Atlantic becomes a food staple in Europe.

1492 Christopher Columbus reaches the Dominican Republic and Haiti.

1534 Jacques Cartier makes the first-known contact with Aboriginal peoples since the Norse in 1000 CE.

PICTURE THIS

Can you imagine what it would be like to have ships full of strange people from a distant land suddenly arrive in your homeland? How would you react as these people moved onto your land? How would you feel if they just took the things they wanted? How would you react if these newcomers asked you to help them find food and teach them how to travel through the wilderness? This is what happened to Aboriginal peoples in North America when Europeans first came here more than 500 years ago.

Can you imagine what it was like when Aboriginal peoples saw these huge European sailing ships for the first time?

TIMELINE

1605 Port Royal in present-day Nova Scotia becomes the first permanent settlement in Canada.

1615 The first missionaries come to New France to convert Aboriginal peoples to the Christian faith.

1639 Missionary Marie de l'Incarnation arrives in New France.

1603 Samuel de Champlain comes to North America.

1608 Champlain sets up a fur-trading post at present-day Quebec City.

1625 The Jesuit missionaries come to New France to convert Aboriginal peoples to Catholicism.

1642 Jeanne Mance arrives at the Catholic colony of Ville-Marie (present-day Montreal).

At the time of **contact**, Aboriginal societies were flourishing across North America. Each culture had learned to adapt to its environment. They had learned what they needed to know to survive. They had developed the skills and invented the tools and technologies they needed to grow and prosper.

Their lifestyles differed according to their environments. Yet all Aboriginal societies enjoyed a special relationship with nature. They depended on nature for their survival. In return, they respected and valued the natural world.

Aboriginal societies based their way of life on the resources that were available to them. Many coastal communities, like those on Vancouver Island, relied on the resources of the sea. Their lives would change, though, with the arrival of Europeans.

TIMELINE

1649 The Huron Nation is destroyed 40 years after Champlain settles at Quebec.

1674 Kateri Tekakwitha settles in the Catholic mission village of Kanawaké.

1871 Canada signs the first of the numbered treaties with First Nations.

1653 Marguérite Bourgeoys comes to New France to do missionary work.

1829 The Beothuk become extinct.

1876 The Indian Act gives the federal government complete control over the lives of Aboriginal peoples.

This scene shows Queen Isabella of Spain welcoming Christopher Columbus. He had just returned from his first voyage across the Atlantic. He brought back some Aboriginal people he had kidnapped. What message does this picture convey? In what ways is this picture biased?

Aboriginal peoples had practiced their traditional ways of life for thousands of years. Then the Europeans arrived. Things were about to change forever.

SETTING THE SCENE

The First Peoples had lived across all parts of North America for thousands of years. They had developed unique societies. Each had its own traditions, customs, values, governments, and religions. Groups traded with one another. They negotiated treaties. They interacted as one nation to another.

Meanwhile, in Europe in the sixteenth century, events were about to take place that would change the lives of Aboriginal peoples forever. The European countries were eager to find a route to Asia across the Atlantic Ocean. At the time, they didn't even know that North America existed. They thought that if they sailed straight across the ocean, they would end up in Asia. They were wrong, of course. They ended up in North America. While they didn't find what they were looking for, they did find many things they wanted. In time, first fish, and then furs, would bring the Europeans here to stay.

TIMELINE

1970 The Aboriginal rights movement in Canada gains momentum.

1980 The Pope beatifies Kateri Tekakwitha, the first Aboriginal saint.

1997 The Supreme Court rules that the oral histories of Aboriginal peoples are valid historical evidence.

1998 Canada issues a formal Statement of Reconciliation apologizing for its past treatment of Aboriginal peoples.

The Nisga'a reach a landmark settlement with the province of British Columbia.

1973 The Supreme Court of Canada recognizes the existence of Aboriginal land claims.

1996 The *Report of the Royal Commission on Aboriginal Peoples* recommends the creation of a House of First Peoples.

1999 The new territory of Nunavut is formally established.

Telling Their Stories

THE WOODLAND STORYTELLER

Neither Europeans nor Aboriginal peoples were prepared for their first encounter with each other. In fact, each side was startled to learn that the other existed. The early encounters were between the Europeans on the fishing boats and the Aboriginal peoples who lived along the eastern shores. For a while, the fish kept bringing the Europeans back to North America. But then they discovered a resource that was far more valuable: fur! Over time, European fur traders pushed deeper into the continent. As they did, they faced new encounters with other Aboriginal nations. Contact would soon change these peoples' lives forever.

View the clip "Contact" (*Canada: A People's History*, Episode 1, 02:00:05 to 02:02:31). How do you think the Woodland Storyteller might have felt seeing a European sailing ship for the first time? How do you think he might have felt about his first encounter with the people on board the ship? What do the other scenes in this opening clip foretell about events to come?

In the seventeenth century, other Europeans came to live in North America, too. They weren't interested in furs, though. They had a different mission. They wanted to spread the beliefs and values of the Christian faith. These **missionaries** settled among the Aboriginal peoples. They tried to convince them to abandon their own spiritual beliefs and become Catholics.

The deadliest thing to happen to Aboriginal peoples because of contact with Europeans was the spread of diseases. The Europeans brought smallpox, influenza, and measles with them to North America. These diseases had not existed here before. Aboriginal peoples had no **immunity** to them. Over time, **epidemics** killed 95 percent of Aboriginal peoples in North America.

Henri Membertu was a Mi'kmaq chief. After the Europeans arrived, he noticed that his people were rapidly disappearing. About 85 percent of the Mi'kmaq Nation died from European diseases.

First Contact examines the period of early contact between Aboriginal peoples and Europeans. What types of societies did Aboriginal peoples have before contact? What first brought Europeans to North America? Why did they stay? How did their actions effect the original inhabitants of this land? What were the consequences?

◀ Playback ▶

1. **In what ways were the values of Aboriginal peoples and Europeans different? Why would these differences affect their relationship?**

2. **How do you think Aboriginal peoples and Europeans communicated when they met for the first time?**

CHAPTER I

THE FIRST PEOPLES

Many Aboriginal cultures, such as the Huron (also known as the Wendat), had complex and well-organized societies. What can you tell about Huron society from this picture?

Before European contact, the Aboriginal peoples of North America had created many unique societies. Each culture had its own religious beliefs and practices. Each had its own traditions and ceremonies. Each had created its own system of government. Each had built its own economy. But while each society was unique, all societies shared a common world view. This was based on a close relationship with the land. Aboriginal peoples believed they were part of the environment. They lived in harmony with nature. They never tried to control it.

SINCE TIME BEGAN

Aboriginal peoples believe they have lived in North America since time began. Each culture has its own creation story. These stories tell how the people came to be here. Some groups believe their people were born from the earth. Others believe they fell from the sky. There are many different creation stories, but they all have one thing in common—they all reveal a deep spiritual connection to the natural world.

From the Sources

The creation stories Aboriginal peoples tell all focus on the relationship between people and nature. But while these stories share this common theme, the details vary from culture to culture.

In this Iroquois (Haudenosaunee) creation story, a woman falls from the sky into the water. She is saved from drowning by the animals that live there.

To Aboriginal peoples, their origins are sacred. How does this image reflect the creation story told here?

Long before the world was created there was an island, floating in the sky, upon which the Sky People lived. They lived quietly and happily. No one ever died or was born or experienced sadness. However, one day one of the Sky Women realized she was going to give birth to twins. She told her husband, who flew into a rage. In the centre of the island there was a tree which gave light to the entire island since the sun hadn't been created yet. He tore up this tree, creating a huge hole in the middle of the island. Curious, the woman peered into the hole. Far below she could see the waters that covered the earth. At that moment her husband pushed her. She fell through the hole, tumbling toward the waters below.

Water animals already existed on the earth, so far below the floating island two birds saw the Sky Woman fall. Just before she reached the waters they caught her on their backs and brought her to the other animals. Determined to help the woman, they dove into the water to get mud from the bottom of the seas. One after another the animals tried and failed. Finally, Little Toad tried and when he reappeared his mouth was full of mud. The animals took it and spread it on the back of Big Turtle. The mud began to grow and grow and grow until it became the size of North America.

Then the woman stepped onto the land. She sprinkled dust into the air and created stars. Then she created the moon and sun.

The Sky Woman gave birth to twin sons. She named one Sapling. He grew to be kind and gentle. She named the other Flint and his heart was as cold as his name. They grew quickly and began filling the earth with their creations.

Sapling created what is good. He made animals that are useful to humans. He made rivers that went two ways and into these he put fish without bones. He made plants that people could eat easily. If he was able to do all the work himself there would be no suffering.

Flint destroyed much of Sapling's work and created all that is bad. He made the rivers flow only in one direction. He put bones in fish and thorns on berry bushes. He created winter, but Sapling gave it life so that it could move to give way to spring. He created monsters which his brother drove beneath the earth.

Eventually Sapling and Flint decided to fight until one conquered the other. Neither was able to win at first, but finally Flint was beaten. Because he was a god Flint could not die, so he was forced to live on Big Turtle's back. Occasionally his anger is felt in the form of a volcano.

An Iroquois creation story

Traditionally, no Aboriginal creation stories were written down. The only written records of the past are found in rock carvings and cave paintings. The carvings are called *petroglyphs*. The paintings are called *pictographs*. What things do you think these petroglyphs show?

The Oral Tradition

Aboriginal peoples tell the stories about their history through their oral traditions. Stories are passed down from one generation to the next. This made language very important.

MANY PEOPLE, MANY LANGUAGES

At the time of contact with Europeans, there were more than 50 Aboriginal groups in North America. They formed many different language families. But within each language family, there were at least 50 different **dialects**.

The most common language was Algonquian. It was spoken in most of eastern and central North America. Along the St. Lawrence River, the people spoke Iroquoian. In the North, the people spoke Eskaleut. In what is today British Columbia, the mountains isolated groups from one another. This led to six different languages in this region.

Today, many of the Aboriginal languages shown on this map are in danger of disappearing. Why is it important for these languages to be preserved?

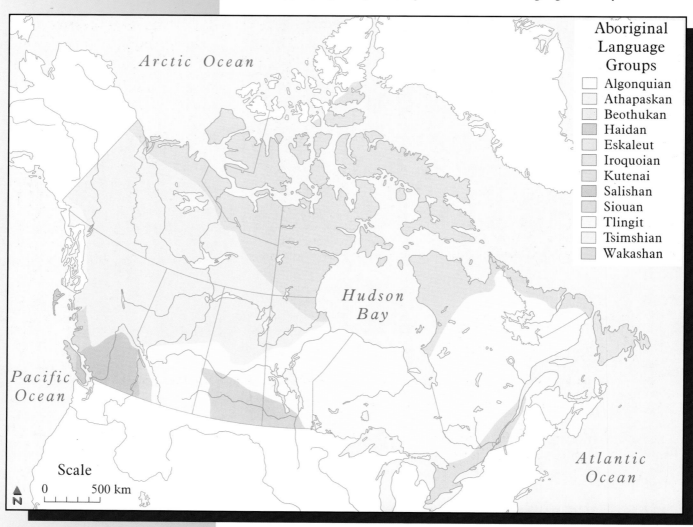

Aboriginal Language Groups
- Algonquian
- Athapaskan
- Beothukan
- Haidan
- Eskaleut
- Iroquoian
- Kutenai
- Salishan
- Siouan
- Tlingit
- Tsimshian
- Wakashan

Arctic Ocean

Hudson Bay

Pacific Ocean

Atlantic Ocean

Scale

0   500 km

N

ABORIGINAL SPIRITUAL BELIEFS

At the time of contact, Aboriginal peoples had deep spiritual and religious beliefs. Their faith had been part of their lives for thousands of years. They had passed on their spiritual beliefs through the stories they told.

Their world view was at the centre of their faith. Aboriginal peoples believe that all living things—plants, animals, and people—have souls. Therefore, all living things are spiritually connected to one another. Aboriginal peoples respected these spirits. They honoured them with special ceremonies. Their religious leaders, called **shamans**, connected the people to the spirits.

The shamans were healers. They knew the secrets of traditional medicines. On the plains, the shamans had a special dance to ward off evil spirits.

◄ Playback ►

1. What does the Iroquois creation story tell you about the relationship between Aboriginal peoples and nature?

2. Draw a pictograph that would tell people living in the future something about your daily life.

Unlike Aboriginal cultures, at the time of first contact, the nations of Europe knew little about democracy or social equality. They were ruled by absolute monarchs. **In France, King Louis XIV had all the power. He could give some power to nobles or military leaders if he wanted to. But the ordinary people of France had no power at all. They had to obey what their rulers told them.**

ABORIGINAL GOVERNMENT

At the time of contact, Aboriginal societies had distinct systems of government. Many of these governments were **democratic**. In most societies, there was **social equality**. All people were treated as equals. The rights of the individual were respected and valued.

Telling Their Stories

DEKANAWIDEH

Dekanawideh created the Iroquois Confederacy. He came to bring peace to the warring Iroquois nations, who were caught up in a long-running cycle of war and revenge. He travelled from nation to nation trying to join them in a peaceful union. He was able to convince them that if they were united, they would be the most powerful force in eastern North America.

View the clip "War" (Canada: A People's History, Episode 1, 01:39:22 to 01:42:15). According to the storyteller, how did the people test Dekanawideh to see if he had supernatural powers? How did the bundle of arrows symbolize the solidarity of the Iroquois Confederacy?

Government in the Iroquois Confederacy

The Iroquois Confederacy was made up of five nations—the Mohawk, the Oneida, the Onondaga, the Cayuga, and the Seneca. (Later, the Tuscarora joined them.) The Iroquois created a complex democracy. In fact, many historians believe that the Iroquois Confederacy is the oldest democracy in the world. Some even say that the governments of Canada and the United States are modelled after it.

Iroquois culture was *matrilineal*—that is, a family was made up of all the people who were descended from the oldest living woman. She was known as the Clan Mother. Each clan was named after an animal, such as the bear clan or the turtle clan. The chiefs were men, but they were chosen by the Clan Mother after she talked things over with the other women of the clan. The Clan Mother held the balance of power. She could remove a chief from his position and appoint a new chief if all the women believed he was not acting wisely.

There were three levels of government in the Iroquois Confederacy. The Village Council was in charge of the affairs of the village. It was made up of men from the clan who were appointed by the clan women. The council was headed by the village chief.

The Council of the Nation dealt with issues that effected the whole Iroquois Confederacy. It was made up of the chiefs from all the villages.

The Grand Council dealt with the big issues within the Confederacy, such as conflicts between villages and going to war with other nations. Each of the five nations had ten representatives on the council. They were chosen by the women of each nation. There was no council chief. Decisions were made by consensus—that is, everyone discussed an issue until they all agreed on a final decision.

C.W. JEFFERYS

Entrance Gate

Creek ↓

Corn Fields

The longhouse was the symbol of the Iroquois Confederacy. A longhouse was home for all the members of an extended family. As many as 50 people lived in a single longhouse.

Different Points of View

Europeans and Aboriginal peoples had different ideas about land ownership. Europeans believed that people owned the land, just as they owned material things, such as clothing and tools. So when they came to North America, they simply claimed the land and its resources for their monarchs. They didn't think about the rights of the Aboriginal peoples who already lived there.

Later, the Europeans signed land treaties with Aboriginal nations. But they had a different understanding of treaties, too. Europeans believed the treaties meant that they *owned* the land. Aboriginal peoples believed the treaties meant that they agreed to *share* the land.

Who Owned the Land?

In keeping with their world view, Aboriginal peoples did not think of the land as something they owned. They believed that the land was there for them to use to meet their daily needs. Their responsibility was to preserve the land so that they could pass it on to the next generation.

Long before Europeans came to North America, Aboriginal nations had been negotiating land **treaties** with one another. The treaties decided who would use the land and how they would use it. Aboriginal societies respected and honoured their treaties.

The Root of All Evil

Aboriginal peoples measured wealth by non-material things. Having spiritual powers and good relationships were more important than having clothes and jewels. They believed that the desire to own material things was the root of all evil. It could lead to jealousy and conflict. Sometimes it could even lead to violence and death. Aboriginal peoples valued material goods only as things to be shared during special ceremonies.

On the west coast, the people held potlatches to give away their material goods. By sharing these things, the host of the potlatch shared the family's material wealth with the other villagers. The potlatch also gave the host power and prestige. The more gifts a family gave away, the more powerful it was.

TRADE RELATIONS

Aboriginal nations traded with one another for thousands of years before Europeans came to North America. In fact, they were skilled traders. They traded things they had in abundance for those things they did not have. Some trade goods were raw materials, such as shells and wood. Other goods, such as tools and jewellery, were made to be traded. In this way, trade spread technologies and ideas across the continent.

ON THE EVE OF CONTACT

Before contact with Europeans, Aboriginal peoples had created successful societies all across North America. But their lives would change forever once Europeans landed on North American shores. In the Mi'kmaq culture, the spirit named Kluskap warned his people of what was to come:

> *There will be white people who come and take this forest away from you. But I am going north, to make a place for you where no white person can ever come. No white person shall ever enter there. And this place will be a place where you may not come while you are alive. You will only travel there after you die on the Earth World.*

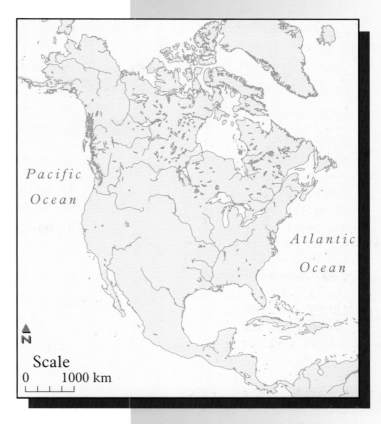

Aboriginal peoples used the many rivers and lakes across North America to transport their goods. This explains why artifacts such as conch shells from the Gulf of Mexico have been found as far north as the Great Lakes.

◀ Playback ▶

1. In what ways was the Iroquois Confederacy democratic? How does this compare with the kind of government in Europe at that time?

2. What was the role of women in the Iroquois Confederacy? What role do you think women in European society had at that time? Why do you think that?

3. (a) How did Aboriginal peoples view land ownership? How did their views compare to those of the Europeans?
   (b) Do you think that these differing view points on land ownership created problems with land treaties?

The Back Story

Prior to European contact, Aboriginal peoples lived in many geographic regions. Each culture developed its own way of life based on the land and natural resources.

The Goal

Working with a partner, do research on the traditional way of life of one cultural group identified on the map.

The Steps

1. Use library resources and the Internet to find information about the cultural group you have selected.
2. Look for information about their traditional ways of life under the following categories: Environment; Economy; Spiritual Beliefs; Government; Social Structure; Housing.
3. Choose a format to present your findings, such as a written or oral report, a poster or bulletin board display, or a video presentation. Include maps and illustrations to show important elements of the culture's lifestyle.

Evaluating Your Work

These are the criteria you should think about as you complete your work. Your work should:
- present enough detailed information so that your audience will gain a real understanding of this culture's lifestyle
- be historically accurate
- be presented in clear language
- be visually appealing

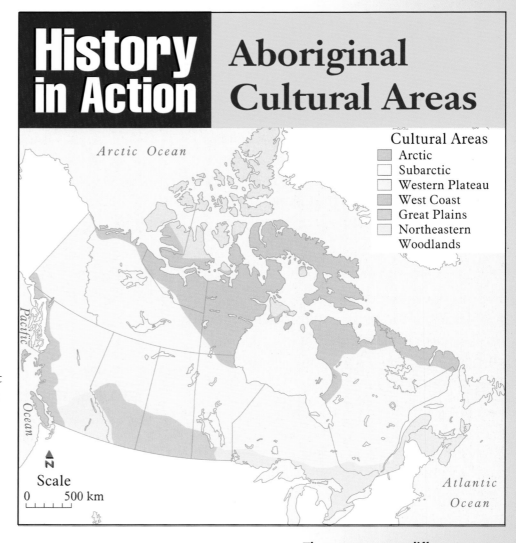

History in Action
Aboriginal Cultural Areas

Arctic Ocean

Pacific Ocean

Scale
0   500 km

Atlantic Ocean

Cultural Areas
- Arctic
- Subarctic
- Western Plateau
- West Coast
- Great Plains
- Northeastern Woodlands

There were many different Aboriginal nations living in North America prior to European contact. Generally, these nations were divided into the six main cultural areas shown on this map.

CHAPTER 2

EARLY EXPLORERS AND SETTLERS

In 1497, John Cabot planted the English flag in North America and claimed the land for King Henry II. Why do you think he did this even though Aboriginal peoples already lived there?

More than 500 years ago, European explorers and sailors set out to cross the unknown waters of the Atlantic Ocean. With their small ships and simple **navigational** tools, they risked capsizing in the rough waters and drowning at sea. Why did these men take such a risk? They were in search of a passage to the Pacific—a passage that would take them to the precious gems, silks, and spices of India and Asia.

THE QUEST FOR WEALTH AND POWER

In Europe, there was great competition for wealth and power. Therefore, many monarchs and merchants were willing to pay the explorers and their voyages. When they set out, they did not expect to find a vast continent between Europe and Asia. But when they did, they were eager to find out what riches this land held. They really wanted to find gold and silver, as the Spanish explorers had in Central and South America in the fifteenth century. This quest would continue to draw European explorers to North America for the next 150 years.

Hundreds of years ago, many people believed that sea serpents lived in the ocean waters, waiting to attack passing ships! Many sailors feared the serpents. Yet they continued to explore the vast oceans.

COLUMBUS BELIEVES THE EARTH IS ROUND

A long time ago, most people believed that the earth was flat. But an Italian explorer named Christopher Columbus thought differently. He believed that the earth was round. He thought that by sailing west across the Atlantic Ocean, he would eventually sail all the way around the earth to Asia. He convinced the Spanish monarch to pay for his expedition. And so in 1492, Columbus set sail in search of a passageway to the Pacific.

When Columbus reached land, he believed he had arrived in India. But he was really on the island that is today the Dominican Republic and Haiti. But the news that he had reached "India" led other explorers to follow in his path.

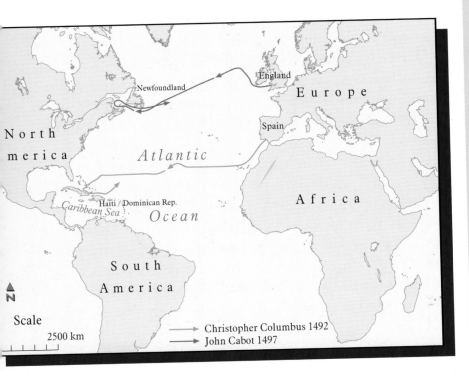

Christopher Columbus 1492
John Cabot 1497

After reaching the Caribbean, Columbus and his three ships sailed around the islands there. In November 1492, he landed at the Dominican Republic and Haiti. Five years later, another explorer, John Cabot, tried to find a passage to Asia by sailing a route farther north.

CABOT CLAIMS A "NEW FOUNDE LAND"

One of the first people to follow Columbus was the Italian explorer Giovanni Caboto—better known as John Cabot. In 1497, he persuaded the English king to finance his trip. Like Columbus, Cabot believed that the earth was round. He thought that if he sailed from a northern location like England, it would be a shorter distance to Asia. When he reached land, he thought he had arrived in China. But he was really somewhere along the North Atlantic coast of North America.

It was John Cabot who first reported seeing so many fish "we could have taken them in baskets." Seeing such an unlimited supply of cod fish, Cabot claimed this "New Founde Land" for England. Upon his return, the English king rewarded Cabot by granting him permission to make another voyage. So the following year, Cabot set sail again. This time he had five ships and a crew of 300 men. No one is sure what happened, but Cabot and his ships were never seen again!

Fish, Fish, Fish

Fish was an important food **staple** in Europe. The population was growing quickly, but many countries could not produce enough food to feed everyone. People also ate fish for religious reasons—in Catholic countries, people were not allowed to eat meat on certain days.

CARTIER MAKES CONTACT

In 1534, Jacques Cartier set sail on the first of three voyages on behalf of the king of France. At first, Cartier's mission was to find a Northwest Passage to Asia. He spent the summer exploring the Gulf of St. Lawrence. He was hoping that he might find a water route across the continent.

During his first trip, Cartier made contact with two Aboriginal groups, the Mi'kmaq and the Iroquois. Both groups were willing to trade their furs for European knives and iron goods. This marked the beginning of what would become the foundation of New France—the fur trade.

Cartier realized that he had found a treasure house of natural resources. To claim the land for France, at Gaspé he set up a cross declaring "Long Live the King of France!" Although he couldn't read French, the Iroquois chief, Donnacona, understood what Cartier was doing. He made angry gestures toward Cartier to show him that the land belonged to his people. But Cartier managed to convince the chief that he had put up the cross simply as a marker to help him find his way.

Jacques Cartier is the first European known to have had direct contact with Aboriginal peoples since the Norse in 1000 CE. What do you think Cartier and his crew would have thought when they first met a group of Aboriginal people? What do you think the Aboriginal people would have thought when they first met Cartier and his crew?

This illustration shows Cartier raising the cross at Gaspé. Do you think this painting shows the Europeans' point of view or the Aboriginal peoples' point of view? What are the clues?

Cartier's second voyage was in 1535. This time, he travelled up the St. Lawrence as far as Hochelaga (present-day Montreal). From the top of a nearby mountain, which he called Mount Royal, Cartier could see where the Ottawa River joined the St. Lawrence. He hoped this might be the route for the Northwest Passage. But the rapids at Hochelaga were too strong for his ships to pass through. Cartier and his crew were forced to return to the Iroquois village of Stadacona (present-day Quebec City). There, in the middle of a bitterly cold winter, 25 of Cartier's men died of scurvy.

When spring came, Cartier returned to France. Before he did, though, he kidnapped some Aboriginal peoples to take with him. Donnacona was one of his captives. Cartier wanted the people to tell the king about the many riches of the continent. Then he was able to convince the king to start a small settlement along the St. Lawrence River. They called it Canada, after the Iroquoian word for village—"kanata."

Aboriginal Medicine

Aboriginal peoples had created many medicines using the forest resources around them. When the Europeans came, the Aboriginals taught them many of these traditional medicines. The Iroquois showed the French how to cure a disease called scurvy using a tea rich in vitamin C. It was made from the bark of a cedar tree.

Telling Their Stories

DONNACONA

The explorers often kidnapped Aboriginal peoples and took them to Europe. There, they presented their captives to the royal courts as proof that there was a vast land they had not known about before.

For those who were kidnapped, it was a terrifying ordeal. They were separated from their families, their people, and the only way of life they knew. Overseas, they were exposed to diseases for which they had no immunity. Few of those who were kidnapped lived to return home.

View the clip "A Star Was Lost in the Sky" (*Canada: A People's History*, Episode 1, 02:29:08 to 02:32:06). Why do you think Donnacona trusted Cartier? What does the reaction of his people outside Cartier's ship tell you about Donnacona's place in Iroquois society? Why do you think Donnacona longed to return home?

This picture shows the French cutting down a cedar tree to make the cure for scurvy.

In 1541, Cartier returned to Stadacona. However, his captives did not return with him—all but one had died from European diseases. Cartier tried to convince the St. Lawrence Iroquois that the people he had kidnapped were alive and well in France. But they distrusted Cartier. They didn't believe his story. Relations between Cartier and the St. Lawrence Iroquois turned hostile.

Near the village of Stadacona, Cartier built two forts for the colonists who were to follow. But after ten months, the harsh weather and tensions with the Iroquois caused Cartier and his group to return to France. When he left, Cartier took with him what he thought were gold and diamonds. But they turned out to be iron pyrite and quartz! Cartier was ridiculed by the members of the king's court. Humiliated, he retired from the sea. He never returned to North America.

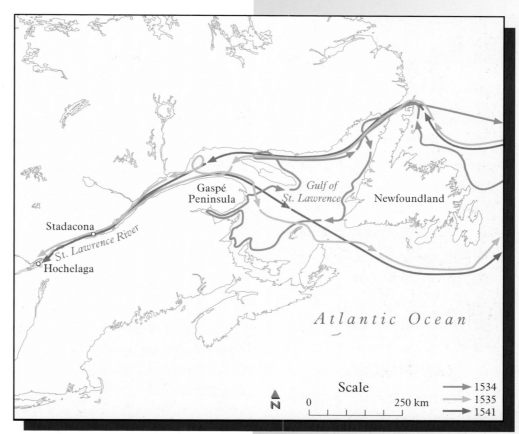

Jacques Cartier was the first European to travel into the interior of the continent along the St. Lawrence River. This map shows his three voyages.

◀ Playback ▶

1. Why was the abundance of fish in the waters off the North Atlantic coast so valuable to Europeans?

2. Do you think the Europeans who kidnapped Aboriginal peoples and took them to Europe believed what they were doing was right? Or do you think they knew it was wrong but did it anyway? Give reasons for your answer.

3. Do you think Cartier should have raised the cross at Gaspé? Give reasons for your answer.

4. Which explorer do you think was the most important—Columbus, Cabot, or Cartier? Explain the reasons for your choice.

Scurvy!

Many of the settlers at Ste. Croix came down with scurvy. Their gums bled and turned black. Then their teeth fell out. They had horrible stomach pains, and their arms and legs became swollen. The settlers were trapped—there was no way to leave the island. By spring, 36 of the 80 settlers had died.

Port Royal was the first permanent settlement in Canada. Today, it is known as Annapolis Royal in Nova Scotia.

DISASTER AT STE. CROIX

In 1603, the French mapmaker and explorer Samuel de Champlain came to North America. He, too, was hoping to find a passage to Asia. He travelled up the St. Lawrence River. But he was forced to turn back at the Lachine Rapids. He returned to France, where he joined an expedition led by a fur trader named Pierre de Monts. In 1604, de Monts, Champlain, and 80 settlers set sail for North America.

The group reached the Bay of Fundy. They decided to spend the winter on a small island they called Ste. Croix. They were not prepared for the winter weather, though. Snow began to fall in the first week of October. By December, ice floes were blocking the river. Although they didn't know it, they were about to endure the longest, coldest winter in years!

In the spring of 1605, the icy waters finally began to melt. Supply ships arrived from France. Although almost half of the settlers were dead, de Monts decided to try again. He moved the settlement across the bay to a small cove on the inner shore of present-day Nova Scotia. They called their new home Port Royal. The settlers built a *habitation*, with a courtyard, palisades, and cannons for protection. They planted a vegetable garden so they could grow food to store for the winter. They also created an active social life to help them cope with the often harsh conditions.

The Order of Good Cheer

In 1606, Champlain decided to create a social club to keep the settlers' spirits up during the long, cold winters. He formed a club called the Order of Good Cheer to hold lively banquets and provide entertainment. Each day, one member of the colony was chosen to be the Grand Master. He was in charge of creating the evening's banquet. The Grand Masters relied on the forests for game such as moose, rabbit, and caribou. The rivers provided them with duck, otter, and salmon. The local Mi'kmaq supplied berries and root vegetables.

After a lavish meal, the men provided their own entertainment. There was singing, dancing, and skits. Everyone enjoyed themselves. It was much different from the first winter they had spent at Ste. Croix!

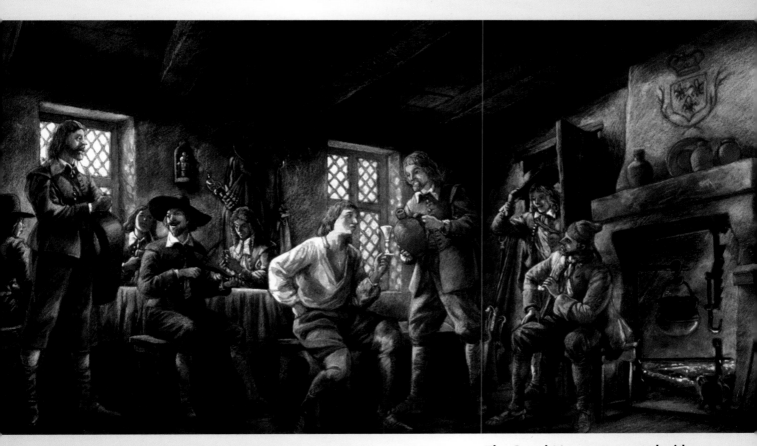

The Grand Masters competed with one another to see who could produce the most lavish banquets. They created such delicacies as moose-meat pie and roasted beaver tail!

From the Sources

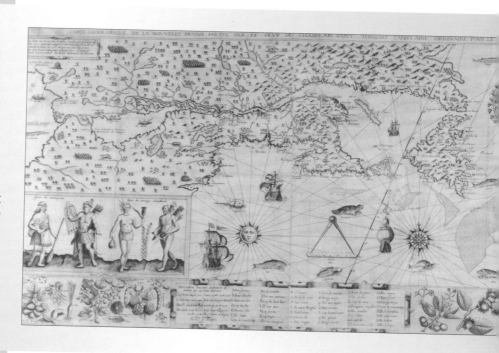

Champlain was an excellent **cartographer**. He made many maps of the lands he travelled, including this map of New France in 1613. The maps helped to convince many merchants in France to support the fur trade in the St. Lawrence Valley.

CHAMPLAIN BUILDS A FORTRESS

In 1607, de Monts lost his fur-trading privileges. So he left Port Royal and sailed with Champlain up the St. Lawrence River. The river narrowed at a place where great cliffs loomed over the water. They decided to settle there, at the abandoned trading post at Stadacona. They called it Quebec, after the Algonquian word "kebec." It means "where the river narrows."

When Cartier visited the St. Lawrence Valley, a group of Iroquois lived there. When Champlain arrived 70 years later, the Iroquois were gone. Now the land was occupied by the Algonquin. No one knows for sure what happened. The Iroquois may have died from the diseases brought over by Cartier and his men on their last voyage in 1535.

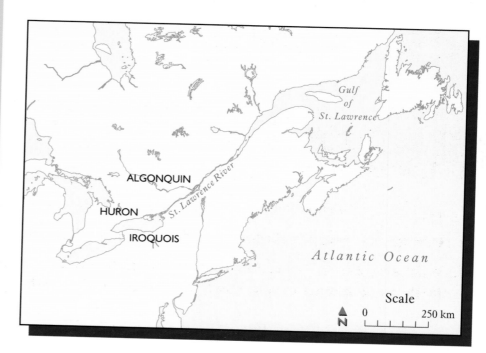

At Quebec, Champlain set out to build a modest fortress to act as the heart of the fur trade. He built his own habitation, modelled after the one at Port Royal. He enlisted the help of the Algonquin and the Huron to obtain furs for the fur trade. But this partnership made the French colonists the enemies of the Iroquois who lived to the south. In the decades ahead, there would be many battles.

Scurvy Strikes Again

The first winter in Quebec was another deadly one for the French. Once again, the settlers became ill with scurvy. Twenty of the 28 men who had accompanied Champlain died. But the few survivors remained to lay the foundations of New France.

The habitation at Quebec was both a fort and a fur-trading post. It planted the seeds of what would become the French Empire in North America.

Playback ▶

1. **Why do you think the colonists were unprepared for winter at Ste. Croix?**

2. **Why do you think the Order of Good Cheer helped the colonists at Port Royal?**

3. **What do you think it would have been like to be one of the early colonists at Quebec? Write a letter home to your family in France describing what your life is like.**

The Back Story

One way to help us understand the past is to try to put ourselves in the place of someone who lived during another time. If we try to think about how a person may have felt or reacted to an event, we come to understand that there are different points of view about the past.

The Goal

With a partner, write an exchange of dialogue between Jacques Cartier and Donnacona. Your conversation should reflect what each man might have said to the other when Cartier raised the cross at Gaspé. Once you have written your dialogue, role-play the scene with your partner.

The Steps

1. Before beginning to write your dialogue, reread the section on the raising of the cross on pages 20 to 21. You might also want to find out more through additional research.
2. Decide who will play each role. Then, think about how you would feel from that person's point of view. Remember to place yourself back in time 500 years.
3. Write down the key points you believe your character would make. Then, discuss these points together with your partner. As you do, begin to write an exchange of dialogue.
4. Finalize your work in the form of a script, then role-play the scene together.

Evaluating Your Work

These are the criteria you should think about as you complete your work. Your work should:

- reflect the attitude of the person you are role-playing
- use persuasive arguments to support your point of view
- show that there are different points of view about the past

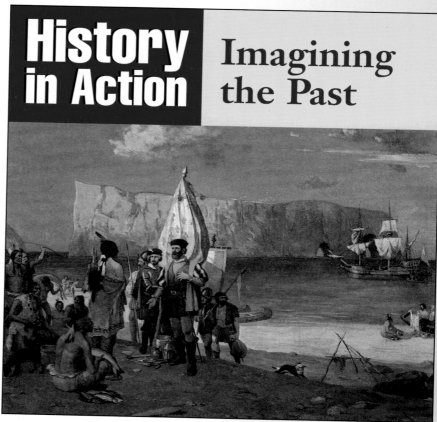

History in Action — Imagining the Past

Jacques Cartier meets the Iroquois chief Donnacona.

CHAPTER 3

ECONOMIC CONTACT

Europeans came to North America in search of adventure. They also came with the hope of making great fortunes! North America promised wealth to those who dared to venture deep into this resource-rich land.

To gain these riches, though, the Europeans needed the help of Aboriginal peoples. Aboriginal peoples had lived here for thousands of years. They knew the land and how to survive on it. Although they didn't know it at the time, their new relationship with the Europeans would change their lives forever.

Trade was the beginning of economic contact between Aboriginal peoples and Europeans. What can you learn about early trade from this painting of Samuel de Champlain trading with Aboriginal peoples?

"SEA SILVER"—THE BOUNTY OF THE COD FISHERY

When they sighted land, the early explorers believed they had arrived at India. In reality, they had reached the North Atlantic coast of North America. They didn't find the gems, silks, and spices they were looking for. Instead, they found riches of a different kind: an abundant supply of "sea silver"—the beautiful, silver-coloured codfish.

The temperature and light on the Grand Banks produce an abundant supply of plankton. These tiny organisms are the main source of food for fish. Use your atlas to locate the Grand Banks.

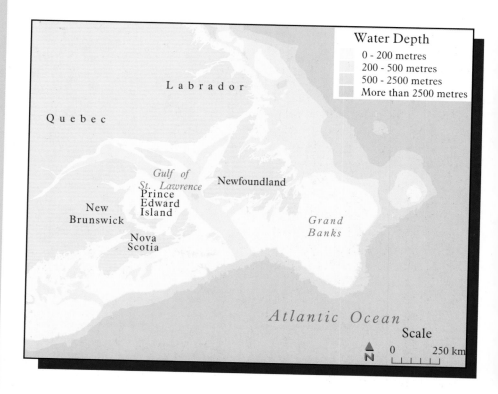

The Fate of the Fishery

Fishing for codfish in the North Atlantic continued for hundreds of years. By 1992, the fish stocks were almost gone. The Canadian government decided to shut down the fishery. It reopened in 1999, but it placed a limit on the number of fish the fishing fleets could catch. But by 2003, the fishery was shut down again. It seems that the abundant supply of fish that Cabot had once found on the Grand Banks may have disappeared forever.

To the explorers, these unexpected riches of the North Atlantic waters were too valuable to ignore. In Europe, fish was an important food staple, but there was not enough supply to meet the demand. The population in Europe was growing. In addition, most Europeans were Catholic. Their church ruled that meat should not be eaten on certain days of the week. On those days, Europeans ate fish.

When news of an ocean teeming with codfish reached Europe, fishing fleets from France, England, Spain, the Netherlands, and Portugal set sail for the Grand Banks. The competition was fierce! Throughout the century, more and more ships reaped the rich harvest of the North Atlantic. By 1600, as many as 800 ships sailed from European ports each year. By the end of the century, codfish was a regular dish on the tables of Europe.

Preserving the Catch

One of the challenges for the fishing fleets was preserving the catch so it didn't spoil on the long journey back to Europe. The French and other European fleets preserved their codfish on board ship. They used a method called wet fishing. The crew netted the fish as they swarmed off the side of the ship. The fish were then split in half and cleaned. Then they were placed in storage bins, between alternating layers of salt.

The fishing crews who used the wet fishing method usually remained on board ship. They only went ashore to get fresh water or to repair their ships. They had little contact with Aboriginal peoples.

The English fleet, on the other hand, did not have much salt. To preserve their fish, they had to take their catch onshore. They built small fishing stations where they used a method called dry fishing to preserve the catch. The fish were cleaned and lightly salted. After a few days, they were cleaned again and placed on wooden racks to dry. Then they were tightly packed and stored on board ship for the journey back to England.

The English used their onshore stations only during the fishing season. In time, though, they built more permanent settlements along the Newfoundland coast. Their presence led to conflict with the Aboriginal peoples who lived there. This would have tragic results for the people known as the Beothuk.

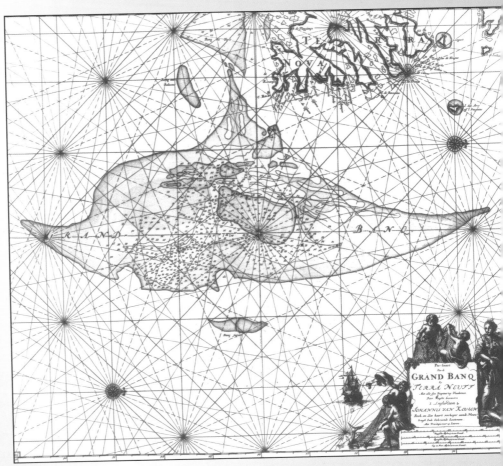

The Dutch created this map of the Grand Banks off Newfoundland in the 1680s.

THE TRAGEDY OF THE BEOTHUK

The story of the Beothuk is one of great tragedy. The Beothuk had lived in Newfoundland for thousands of years. For most of the year, they lived along the coast. They fished for salmon in the rivers and hunted seals offshore. In the fall, they moved inland to hunt caribou.

The arrival of English and Irish settlers on the Newfoundland coast changed this way of life. The Beothuk were afraid of the Europeans. They tried to avoid contact with them. But then the Europeans set up their fishing villages along the coast. The villages blocked the Beothuks' access to the sea. Then the fishers began stringing nets across the rivers. This disrupted the salmon migration and cut off the Beothuks' food supply. The Beothuk could no longer pursue their traditional marine lifestyle. They were forced to move inland, where they had to find new ways to survive.

Telling Their Stories

SHAWNADITHIT

In 1823, a group of English fur traders came upon the last Beothuk family in Newfoundland—a mother and her two daughters. They were starving and near death. The mother and one daughter soon died of tuberculosis. The other daughter was named Shawnadithit. She survived for another five years. During this time, she lived in St. John's. There, an English merchant named John Cormack encouraged her to tell the story of her people. In the years before her own death from tuberculosis in 1829, Shawnadithit told the Beothuks' story through her drawings. Upon her death, the Beothuk culture disappeared for all time.

View the clips "Shawnadithit #1" and "Shawnadithit #2: Massacre" (*Canada: A People's History*, Episode 1, 01:00:19 to 01:03:43 and 01:51:32 to 01:56:17). Why do you think it is important to learn about the history and fate of the Beothuk people from Shawnadithit? How did misunderstanding and fear lead to the tragedy of the Beothuk?

The Beothuk did not find safety in the forests, though. The fur trade expanded into Newfoundland. This increased contact between the Beothuk and the Europeans. The Beothuk tried to remain out of sight, but this made the Europeans suspicious. They were afraid of people they did not know or understand. So the colonists hunted the Beothuk. Many Beothuk men, women, and children were killed on sight.

Violence was not the only thing that was killing the Beothuk, though. Many people were dying from starvation as their food supplies were cut off. Others were dying from European diseases for which they had no immunity. The Beothuk population was quickly being wiped out. By 1829, contact between Aboriginal peoples and European settlers had taken the ultimate toll. The Beothuk had become extinct.

A Lack of Justice

For many years, it was legal to kill the Beothuk. It wasn't until 1769 that the murder of Beothuk peoples was made illegal. But the killings didn't stop, and no settlers were ever arrested.

Shawnadithit used her artistic skills to tell the story of the Beothuk people and their tragic fate.

The Basques

The Basques have lived in the Pyrenees Mountains between northern Spain and south-western France for thousands of years. In the late sixteenth century, as many as 1000 Basque whalers came to Red Bay on the coast of Labrador each year.

THE ANCIENT PURSUIT OF WHALING

Cod was not the only resource of value along the North Atlantic. By the second half of the sixteenth century, the Europeans' activities had expanded to include whaling. Whaling was an important industry in Europe. Whales were a valuable source of oil. The whaling industry also provided jobs for many people.

The Basque people were the first Europeans to exploit the whale resources off Newfoundland and Labrador. They did most of their whaling at a place called Red Bay on the coast of Labrador. There, they could hunt whales as they **migrated**.

This display at the Canadian Museum of Civilization shows some of the tools the early European whalers used.

The Whale Hunt

Whale hunting was highly organized. The European whalers sailed the waters looking for whales. When they sighted one, they wounded the huge creature by throwing a harpoon into its back. Then, they followed the animal, now weak from its injury, until it surfaced above water. Then, the whalers used spears to inflict the final deadly blows.

Once the animal was dead, the whalers hauled the carcass back to the whaling station. There, a factory was set up to turn the whale blubber into oil. Then, the oil was stored in barrels and loaded on board ship to await the journey back to Europe.

At the end of the summer, most whaling ships returned home. But some daring whalers sometimes decided to stay longer. Many of them got trapped by ice and were forced to spend the winter huddling for warmth in their ships. Many whalers died this way.

Whale hunting could be very dangerous. What does this image tell you about some of these dangers?

WHALING IN THE ARCTIC

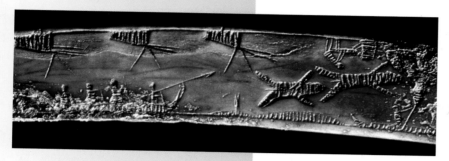

The Inuit hunted whales using harpoons and spears. They navigated the icy waters on boats made from animal skins. The scenes engraved on this ivory bow show some hunters paddling a umiak in pursuit of a whale.

By the late seventeenth century, the whale population around Newfoundland was on the decline. So European whalers began hunting in the Arctic. The Inuit had hunted whales there for thousands of years. Whales were an important part of their **subsistence** economy. Whale meat provided the Inuit with food. The bones were carved into tools. The blubber was melted down for oil. Almost no part of the whale was wasted.

WHALING EFFECTS THE INUIT

The arrival of European whalers in the Arctic greatly affected the Inuit. The whalers hired the Inuit as hunters, navigators, and crew on board ship. They traded European goods, including alcohol, for animal skins and other goods. As the whaling industry expanded, it strained the natural resources of the Arctic. Caribou herds were wiped out as the animals were killed to provide meat to feed the whalers. Many Inuit began to rely on the whaling economy to meet their daily needs. Contact also led to deadly epidemics as the Europeans brought diseases to the Inuit. The Inuit had no immunity to fight these diseases. As a result, thousands of people died.

A Whaling Ban

Today, whaling is banned in Canadian waters, except by the Inuit who hunt whales for subsistence. Why do you think the government banned whaling?

◄Playback►

1. **Why do you think the establishment of English fishing stations on shore led to conflict with Aboriginal peoples? How do you think Aboriginal peoples might have felt to have strangers move onto their land?**

2. **Why did the Inuit hunt whales? How is this different from European whale hunting?**

3. **Hundreds of years ago, why do you think the whalers hunted until there were hardly any whales left? Are you aware of any similar situations with other wildlife resources today?**

THE FUR TRADE BEGINS

The fur trade began in Atlantic Canada in the early 1500s. At first, it was a spin-off of the fishing and whaling industries. The Europeans had to stay onshore for several weeks as they dried their fish catch or processed their whale oil. They wanted to have a good relationship with the Aboriginal peoples who lived there. The Aboriginal peoples wanted the Europeans' iron tools and utensils. They offered to trade them for furs and meat.

At first, this exchange was good for both sides. For Aboriginal peoples, European tools made some of their daily tasks easier. For the Europeans, trade had two benefits. One was the lure of money—they knew they could sell the furs back in Europe for huge profits. The second benefit was a practical one—they needed Aboriginal peoples to teach them how to survive in the harsh and unfamiliar land.

Jacques Cartier was one of the first Europeans to meet Aboriginal peoples in North America.

From the Sources

In 1534, Jacques Cartier recorded his first encounter with Aboriginal peoples. The French were anchored at Chaleur Bay off the Gulf of St. Lawrence. They were approached by a group of Mi'kmaq waving furs on the ends of poles.

The next day, some of the Indians came in nine canoes to the point at the mouth of the cove where we lay anchored with our ships. And being informed of their arrival we sent our two long-boats to the point where they were.... As soon as they saw us they began to run away, making signs to us that they had come to barter with us; and held up some furs of small value, with which they clothe themselves. We likewise made signs to them that we wished them no harm, and sent two men on shore to offer them some knives and other iron goods, and a red cap to their chief.... [They] showed a marvelously good pleasure in possessing and obtaining these iron wares and other commodities....

The Fur Trade Expands

The demand for furs in Europe grew quickly. As it did, the focus of European exploration moved from the coast to the interior. By 1600, the St. Lawrence River was set to become the centre of the fur trade.

In the early days, Tadoussac was the main trading post. There, French traders met with the Algonquin and Montagnais peoples. They exchanged European iron goods for thick and shiny animal furs.

In 1608, Samuel de Champlain arrived in New France. He had a plan to set up a new trading post. He wanted to move farther inland, away from the competition at Tadoussac. He set sail down the St. Lawrence River. When he reached the abandoned Iroquois village of Stadacona, he decided to set up his new fur-trading post. He called this new fort Quebec.

The Coureurs de Bois

At Quebec, Champlain wanted to expand the fur trade. He also wanted to maintain his **alliances** with the Algonquin and the Huron. So he sent out young French men to live among these allies. The men were encouraged to learn the language and customs of the people. Champlain also wanted them to travel with Aboriginal hunters into their traditional hunting grounds. Eventually, some of these young men became unlicenced fur traders. They came to be known as *coureurs de bois*—"runners of the woods."

The Plot Against Champlain

Basque whalers also gathered at Tadoussac. The competition between the Basques and the French was fierce. Among Champlain's men was a traitor named Jean Duval. He organized a plot with the Basques to **assassinate** Champlain. Then the Basques could take over the trading post at Quebec. But Champlain found out about the plot and quickly put an end to it. He captured Duval and hanged him for **treason**.

For many Aboriginal peoples, their first contact with Europeans was with the *coureurs de bois.*

Étienne Brûlé

Étienne Brûlé travelled widely with the Huron. He was likely the first European to see Lakes Ontario, Huron, and Superior.

One of the most daring of the French explorers was Étienne Brûlé. Brûlé arrived in New France as a teenager in 1610. He became part of a unique cultural exchange between the Huron and the French. Both sides accepted their cultural differences and were eager to learn more about one another. A young Huron boy was sent to live in France for a year. In return, Brûlé was to spend a year living among the Huron. He helped to forge an important alliance between the French and the Huron. He learned the Huron language and customs and acted as an interpreter.

When the year was up, Brûlé decided to remain with the Huron. He lived and travelled with his adopted people for the next 20 years. At one time he was captured by the Iroquois, but he managed to escape.

Eventually, Brûlé's spirit of adventure caught up with him. He began dealing with a group of English traders and their Aboriginal allies. Champlain accused him of treason. In 1635, Brûlé returned to Huronia. He was executed by the Huron for betraying them.

From the Sources

Champlain recorded details about the battle with the Iroquois in his journal.

I saw the enemy come out of their barricade…. They came slowly to meet us with a gravity and calm which I admired; and at their head were three chiefs. Our Indians likewise advanced in similar order, and told me that those who had the three big plumes were the chiefs and I was to do what I could to kill them….

The Iroquois were much astonished that two men should have been killed so quickly. As I was reloading…one of my companions fired a shot…. Seeing their chiefs dead, they lost courage and took to flight into the depth of the forest.

MILITARY ALLIANCES SECURE THE FUR TRADE

In 1609, the Montagnais, the Algonquin, and the Huron urged Champlain to join them in a raid against their enemy, the Iroquois. Champlain wanted to maintain good relations with his trading partners, so he agreed. In July 1609, Champlain and a few of his men joined forces with the three Aboriginal nations. They headed south towards Iroquois lands. A month later, the battle with the Iroquois began.

With the French as their allies, the Montagnais, the Algonquin, and the Huron had a unique advantage: European weapons. The French fired their guns at the oncoming Iroquois. They killed several men. Startled by the power of the weapons, the remaining Iroquois scattered into the woods.

The battle at Ticonderoga was the first of many that Champlain and his men fought alongside their allies. Over the next six years, Champlain took part in many raids against the Iroquois.

A COSTLY ALLIANCE

The battle against the Iroquois made the French military partners with the Montagnais, the Algonquin, and the Huron. But it also dragged them into the long-standing rivalry and hostility that existed between these nations and the Iroquois. Now, the French were also the bitter enemies of the Iroquois. Their alliance with the Huron was intended to ensure the success of the fur trade. But conflict with the Iroquois threatened to destroy it!

For the next 100 years, New France was under a state of siege. Both sides launched surprise attacks against one another. There were periods of intense battles, followed by short-lived **truces**. All the while, the fur trade remained at the heart of the conflict.

By the middle of the seventeenth century, the Iroquois had become dependent on European goods, including weapons. To obtain these goods, they had to supply furs to their Dutch trading partners in northern New York. But there were few beavers left there. So the Iroquois needed to obtain furs farther north, above the lands controlled by the Huron. To get to the furs, though, they had to eliminate the enemy.

DEATH OF A NATION

The Huron population was already weakened by an enemy of another kind: disease. Missionaries from France brought smallpox, measles, and influenza to their post at Sainte-Marie-among-the-Hurons. Between 1634 and 1640, epidemics swept through the Huron population.

The time was right for the Iroquois to take over Huron trade. In 1649, they launched a full-scale attack against their enemy. It was a devastating invasion. Village after village was destroyed. Most of the Huron who had survived the epidemics were killed in the raids. A few hundred Huron managed to flee to the north and to Quebec. But the place called Huronia ceased to exist. A mere 40 years after the arrival of Champlain, the once powerful Huron Nation had disappeared.

Shifting Trade Partnerships

As the fur trade moved farther inland away from the St. Lawrence Valley, the Huron replaced the Montagnais as France's main trading partner. The Huron no longer used the Montagnais as the go-betweens. Now they worked directly with French fur traders. But the Algonquin still controlled the Ottawa River. They began charging tolls on the traders' canoes as they passed through.

The Iroquois raids wiped out the Huron Nation.

THE VOYAGEURS TRAVEL DEEPER INTO THE CONTINENT

The *coureurs de bois* were the first French traders to travel into the forests in search of furs. In time, though, the demand for fur increased while the supply along the St. Lawrence River began to dwindle. This led to a new phase of the fur trade. Young French adventurers known as the *voyageurs* paddled their canoes deeper into the continent. They carried supplies of European goods with them to trade with Aboriginal peoples. They returned to the St. Lawrence the next year bearing huge bundles of furs.

The Brandy Trade

One of the goods the *voyageurs* traded was brandy. Missionaries were against trading brandy for furs because of the negative impact alcohol had on Aboriginal communities. But the fur traders believed brandy was a necessary trading item. The English and Dutch traders in the south traded brandy for furs. The French traders believed they had to trade alcohol, too, if they were going to compete. And so the brandy trade flourished in New France.

The *voyageurs* were a vital link in the fur trade. They paddled great canoes loaded with trading goods and furs. They explored new territories and met many Aboriginal cultures.

THE IMPACT OF THE FUR TRADE ON ABORIGINAL PEOPLES

As the *voyageurs* travelled farther inland, they expanded the impact that the fur trade had on Aboriginal peoples. Aboriginal economies were threatened by the increasing pressure to meet the demand for beaver pelts for the European hat industry. As a result, the people came to rely more and more on the European goods they received in exchange for the pelts.

The fur trade also damaged the spiritual connection that Aboriginal peoples had with nature. They never wasted any part of the animals they hunted. But the number of animals that were killed for the fur trade led to a drastic drop in the animal population. The people could no longer maintain their delicate balance with nature.

Playback ▶

1. Imagine that you are a young *coureur de bois* living in New France. What do you think would be the most exciting part of your work? What would be the most difficult?

2. Why was it important for the French to secure an alliance with the Huron? What impact did this alliance have?

3. How significant was the role of the fur trade in destroying the Huron Nation? Explain your answer.

4. Why were beaver pelts in such high demand? Where were the pelts made into felt hats?

5. Whom do you think benefited more from first contact, Europeans or Aboriginal peoples? Give reasons for your answer.

The Back Story

Visual evidence, such as an historical painting, can be an important source of information. It may reveal many clues about past events and other cultures. It may allow you to see such things as clothing styles, technologies, and the physical environment. We need to be careful when we use this type of evidence, though. It is important to remember that you see what the artist *wants* you to see. Therefore, it is important to look for **bias** when viewing visual evidence.

The Goal

In this activity, you are to analyze the painting shown here to find out what it reveals about Jacques Cartier and his meeting with Aboriginal peoples at Hochelaga.

This painting depicts Jacques Cartier and some of his men meeting with the Iroquois at Hochelaga (present-day Montreal).

The Steps

1. Study the painting carefully. Identify the action that is taking place.
2. Look at the painting two or three times and make notes about the details of the scene.
3. Based on the evidence in this painting, write an account of what life was like for the fur traders. In your account, speculate about the kinds of things Cartier and the Iroquois at Hochelaga may have talked about.

Evaluating Your Work

These are the criteria you should think about as you evaluate your work. Your work should:

- show that you have studied the painting carefully and looked for the details
- present an accurate account of the meeting place based on the evidence in the painting
- demonstrate some ideas about what might have been important to Cartier and the Iroquois
- be written in clear and concise language, with correct spelling and grammar

CHAPTER 4

AN AGE OF FAITH

Religion was important during the Age of Faith. This can be seen in many works of art created during that time. In this painting, the woman is showing a religious painting to an Aboriginal person as she points up to heaven. Both figures are wearing the *fleur-de-lis*, the symbol of France. What do you think is the message in this painting?

At the time of European exploration, the Catholic Church controlled most of the values, beliefs, and traditions in Europe. Most Europeans followed the Catholic faith. They did not understand—or tolerate—the beliefs of others. They believed that their faith was the one true religion.

Between 1517 and 1555, some people began to question the power of the Catholic Church. This movement was called the Protestant Reformation. It grew to become a powerful force in Europe. The leaders of the Reformation demanded changes in the Church. When the changes didn't happen, many people broke away from the Catholic Church. They created their own religions. These became known as the Protestant or Reformed religions.

SPREADING CHRISTIANITY AROUND THE WORLD

Many Catholic leaders believed these new churches threatened the power of the Catholic Church. So the monarchs of France, Spain, and Portugal launched the Counter-Reformation. Their goal was to spread the beliefs and values of the Catholic Church around the world. In the 1600s, European missionaries sailed to New France to spread the Catholic faith.

Two Different World Views

The world views of Aboriginal peoples and Europeans at the time of first contact were very different. Aboriginal peoples believed that nature was a "web of life." All living things were equal partners. They lived in harmony with one another; no one living thing controlled another. The European Christian view saw the world as a pyramid. People were at the top. They dominated all other things beneath them. Which world view do you agree with? Give reasons for your answer.

The Aboriginal world view: the world is a "web of life."

The European world view: the world is a pyramid.

The Missionaries Come to New France

The first missionaries in New France were the Récollets. Samuel de Champlain arranged for these priests to come to the colony in 1615. The priests wanted Aboriginal peoples to give up their own beliefs, language, and culture. They wanted them to become Catholics and to adopt the French way of life.

At first, Aboriginal peoples did not want the priests there. But Champlain insisted they had to stay—no missionaries, no trade! So the people agreed to have the priests live among them. But they refused to abandon their own spiritual beliefs for a religion that had no meaning to them. After a few years, the Récollets gave up and returned to France.

Ten years later, another group of missionaries came to New France. They were called the Jesuits. They also wanted Aboriginal peoples to become Catholics. At first, the Jesuits tried to convert the Algonquin. But the Algonquin lived a **semi-nomadic** lifestyle based on the seasons as they hunted game and gathered plants and berries. So the Jesuits decided to settle among the Huron. The Huron were farmers, so they remained in one place to tend to their crops.

This map shows the location of Huronia and Sainte-Marie-among-the-Hurons. What do you think the advantages of this site were?

The Religious Practices of the Hurons

In the Huron Nation, religion was part of daily life. For example, after a hunt, the people showed respect for the soul of the dead animal by refusing to give its bones to their dogs. They also believed that religious guidance came to them through their dreams. If they interpreted their dreams correctly, they would make good choices in their lives.

Aboriginal peoples were not the only ones who didn't want the priests in New France. Many of the fur traders didn't want them there, either. They thought they interfered in their business with Aboriginal hunters.

At first, the Huron tolerated the Jesuits. They wanted to keep their trade and military alliance with the French. But then the Jesuits began to persuade some Huron to convert. They made special agreements with them. People who were **baptized** as Catholics were given better trade deals. They were rewarded with the chance to buy guns. In return, the Huron had to abandon their traditional rituals and customs. This included their **burial rites**. These rites were an important part of Huron culture. They had practiced them for thousands of years.

The Huron Carol

Music had a special place in Aboriginal religions. The Jesuits used music to help them persuade people to convert. Jean de Brébeuf was one of the Jesuit priests at Sainte-Marie-among-the-Hurons. He wrote "The Huron Carol." It combined Huron words with French folk music. The song is likely the first Canadian hymn.

T'was in the moon of winter time
When all the birds had fled,
That mighty Gitchi Manitou
Sent angel choirs instead;
Before their light the stars grew dim
And wand'ring hunters heard the hymn:
"Jesus your King is born,
Jesus is born: In excelsis gloria!"

Within a lodge of broken bark
The tender Babe was found
A ragged robe of rabbit skin
Enwrapped His Beauty 'round;
And as the hunter braves drew nigh
The angel song rang loud and high:
"Jesus your King is born,
Jesus is born: In excelsis gloria!"

The earliest moon of winter time
Is not so round and fair
As was the ring of glory on
The helpless Infant there.
The chiefs from far before Him knelt
With gifts of fox and beaver pelt.
"Jesus your King is born,
Jesus is born: In excelsis gloria!"

O children of the Forest free,
O sons of Manitou,
The Holy Child of earth and heaven
Is born today for you.
Come kneel before the radiant Boy
Who brings you beauty, peace, and joy.
"Jesus your King is born,
Jesus is born: In excelsis gloria!"

Playback ▶

1. How did the Aboriginal view that all living things have a soul affect their relationship with nature?

2. Why do you think Europeans believed that the Catholic faith should be spread around the world? How would you feel if people from a distant land tried to change your beliefs?

3. Why did the Jesuits decide to focus their attention on the Huron rather than the Algonquin?

4. In what ways does "The Huron Carol" try to make connections between the teachings of the Church and life in the wilderness?

The work of Jeanne Mance is honoured in many public dedications to her. This stained-glass window is in l'Hôtel-Dieu, the hospital she built in Montreal.

RELIGIOUS WOMEN OF NEW FRANCE

Priests were not the only ones trying to spread the beliefs of the Catholic Church. Many religious women also came to New France. Among them was a nurse named Jeanne Mance. She was a member of a religious group called the Société Notre-Dame de Montréal. This group was formed in France in 1640. Their goal was to build a missionary colony in New France. The colony's goal was to convert Aboriginal peoples to the Catholic faith.

Mance arrived in New France in 1642 to work in the colony they called Ville-Marie. (Today, we know it as Montreal.) Mance's first goal was to build a hospital. She called it l'Hôtel-Dieu—the hostel of God.

Throughout her life, Jeanne Mance worked hard to make sure the colony was a success. She crossed the Atlantic Ocean many times when the mission was in trouble to get money to keep things going. Because of her efforts, Jeanne Mance is said to be one of the founders of Montreal.

In 1653, Marguérite Bourgeoys left a comfortable life in France to join Jeanne Mance in Ville-Marie. Bourgeoys was a teacher. She dedicated her life in Ville-Marie to helping the poor and struggling settlers. She opened the first school in an abandoned stable in 1658. Later, she opened three more schools. She taught such things as cooking and sewing as well as reading and writing.

Marguérite Bourgeoys also founded the Sisters of the Congregation of Notre-Dame. The nuns travelled through New France, offering help and guidance to the settlers. When the *filles du roi* came to New France, Bourgeoys helped these young women settle in their new home.

Both Jeanne Mance and Marguérite Bourgeoys were devoted to their work. They focused all of their energy on helping others. These women made important contributions to the growth and development of New France.

Marguérite Bourgeoys and the Sisters of the Congregation of Notre-Dame travelled on foot, on horseback, and in canoes to help the settlers in New France. The Order still exists today.

Telling Their Stories

MARIE DE L'INCARNATION

One of the best-known religious women in New France was Marie de l'Incarnation. She was born Marie Guyart in Tours, France, in 1599. By the time she was 19, Marie was a widow with a young son. She moved in with her sister's family and worked in her brother-in-law's shipping business. Marie showed a keen business sense. Soon, she was running the company.

At the same time, Marie displayed another unique quality as a **mystic**. She heard voices and saw visions. She believed these were calling her to religious service. So she placed her son in a boarding school. Then she took her vows with the Ursulines, a religious order for women. In the convent, she took the name Marie de l'Incarnation.

In 1639, Marie persuaded a wealthy woman to sponsor her and two other nuns to go to New France. Once there, she opened the first girls' school. She set up a convent to train other nuns. She translated religious prayers into the Iroquoian language. She wrote French-Iroquoian and French-Algonquian dictionaries. Marie also recorded information about life in New France through the many letters she wrote home to France.

View the clip "A Holy City in the Wilderness" (*Canada: A People's History*, Episode 2, 11:07:48 to 11:12:15). Why did Marie de l'Incarnation leave her son to enter the Ursuline convent? Why did she decide to go to New France? What was so important about the role of the nuns in New France?

Kateri Tekakwitha: Lily of the Mohawks

This oil painting is the oldest portrait of Kateri Tekakwitha. It hangs in St. Francis Xavier Church in the Kanawaké Mohawk Reserve.

Kateri Tekakwitha was born in 1656 in what is today New York State. Her mother was a member of the Algonquin Nation. Her father was a Mohawk chief. According to the traditions of her culture, Kateri was a member of her mother's Algonquin Nation.

While still a child, Kateri's parents and brother died when a smallpox epidemic swept through the Mohawk Valley. Kateri survived the disease. But it left her badly scarred and physically weak for the rest of her life.

After her parents died, Kateri was adopted by her uncle and his wife. But she was attracted to the teachings of the Jesuits. Soon, she adopted their faith. Kateri worked hard to help her family. But she observed the teachings of the Church and refused to work on Sundays. She also refused to marry. She preferred to commit herself to a religious life. Because of this, Kateri was scorned by her family and her community.

It was too hard for Kateri to practice her faith in the Mohawk Valley. With the help of some Jesuits, she left her home in 1674. She settled in the mission village of Kanawaké on the St. Lawrence River, near present-day Montreal. She was accepted into the convent there. She devoted herself to studying the Catholic faith. But Kateri remained weak and fragile from the effects of smallpox years earlier. In 1680, she died at the age of 24.

After her death, Kateri became a symbol of hope in the Catholic Church. In 1980, she was **beatified** by the Pope. Today, people visit the Kanawaké Reserve to honour Kateri Tekakwitha.

DEATH, FEAR, AND RESENTMENT

The Jesuits were able to convert some of the Huron to the Catholic faith. But in the process, they divided Huron society. On one side were those who had converted. On the other side were those who had refused.

The social division grew wider as deadly diseases like smallpox, measles, and influenza swept through Huronia. Aboriginal peoples had no immunity to these diseases. Thousands of people died. The Huron were afraid and angry. They believed the Jesuits were poisoning them.

As the death toll rose, the missionaries increased their efforts to convert the Huron. They convinced many who were dying that only those who were baptized would go to heaven. So many of these people agreed to be baptized. Then they would go to heaven and be with dead relatives who had been baptized.

The shamans were against what the Jesuits were doing. They wanted to preserve the Huron's sacred burial rites. They convinced many Huron to reject the Jesuits and to maintain the burial customs they had practiced for thousands of years.

From the Sources

The Huron believed that the Jesuits were calling upon evil spirits to help them spread the diseases among their people. One Huron woman described the Huron's point of view:

The black robes are casting spells on us and making us die. They came into a village where everyone was doing just fine: as soon as they arrived, everyone died. They went to visit some cabins in other settlements, and it is only the places where they never set foot that have been spared death and illness. Unless they are quickly put to death, they will end up devastating the country, so that neither young nor old will live there any longer.

Aboriginal peoples called the Jesuits the "black robes." Do you think this illustration was created by a European or an Aboriginal person? What makes you think so?

Sainte-Marie-among-the-Hurons

Between 1639 and 1649, Sainte-Marie-among-the-Hurons was the headquarters of the Jesuits. The settlement included a chapel, a cemetery, and a hospital. The site was destroyed in 1649.

But during the ten years it existed, Sainte-Marie-among-the-Hurons planted the roots of French culture in North America.

Sainte-Marie consisted of 20 buildings. For protection, the buildings were surrounded by a palisade.

The Huron taught the Jesuit how to grow corn, beans, and squash. They also showed them which wild fruits and berries were safe to eat.

The Jesuits were assisted by men called *donnés* who did work around the mission. They didn't receive wages. Instead, they were provided with food, clothing, and shelter.

A NATION DESTROYED

By 1649, the Huron Nation was extremely weak. Their great enemy, the Iroquois, had been raiding their villages throughout the 1640s. Thousands of people had been killed. By 1649, disease and warfare had taken their toll. More than half the Huron population was dead.

The Huron had little power left to defend themselves. They were more vulnerable than ever to the Iroquois. In 1649, their enemy launched the final attack. The Jesuits decided to burn Sainte-Marie-among-the-Hurons and join the fleeing Huron. Hundreds of people were killed. The once great and powerful Huron Nation had been destroyed.

Today, a reconstruction of Sainte-Marie-among-the-Hurons sits on the original site near Georgian Bay, Ontario.

◀ Playback ▶

1. (a) **Why do you think religious women left France to settle in New France?**
   (b) **What were some of the challenges these women would have faced?**
   (c) **How important were the contributions these women made to New France?**

2. **Imagine you are Kateri Tekakwitha. Write a journal entry that reflects what it feels like to be torn between your cultural traditions and your religious beliefs.**

3. **Create a web diagram to show the factors that combined to destroy the Huron Nation.**

The Back Story

One of the ways historians have learned about New France is by reading first-hand accounts, such as letters and journals, written by the people who lived there. These accounts are called **primary sources**.

During the Age of Faith, the Jesuits recorded many of their thoughts about Huronia and its people. These works are known as the *Jesuit Relations*. The section of a letter written by Father Charles Lalemant in 1627, shown at right below, reveals some of the missionaries' thoughts about bringing the Christian faith to Aboriginal peoples.

The Goal

This activity asks you to act as an historian as you analyze a primary source document from the *Jesuit Relations*.

The Steps

1. Read the document on the right carefully. As you read, jot down the key points.

2. Use a dictionary to look up the meaning of any words you don't understand. In your notes, write the word and a brief definition beside it.

3. Identify any words or phrases that you think reflect the writer's bias.

4. In a brief statement, explain whether or not this document is a valuable source of evidence. Give reasons for your answer.

Evaluating Your Work

These are the criteria you should think about as you complete your work. Your work should:

- show that you have read and understood the primary source document
- define any words you didn't understand
- present evidence of bias
- present arguments to show the value of the document as a source of evidence

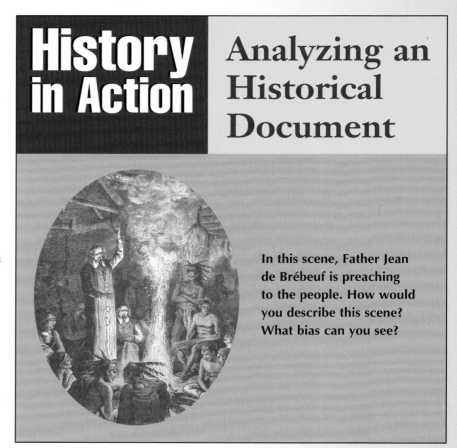

History in Action

Analyzing an Historical Document

In this scene, Father Jean de Brébeuf is preaching to the people. How would you describe this scene? What bias can you see?

... They attach great faith to their dreams. Some of them will tell you two days before the arrival of ships the hour of their arrival and will tell you nothing more except that they have seen it in their sleep. These people are reputed ... to be able to speak to the Devil. Their conversion will give us no little difficulty. Their ... lazy lives, their rude minds which can scarcely grasp things, the [few] words ... they have to explain our mysteries because they have never had any form of divine worship, will tax our wits. Yet we do not lose courage, thank God, because we trust in this truth that God will not take so much account of the fruit we produce as of the good disposition and the labour we undertake....

A letter from Father Charles Lalemant, 1627, translated by Dr. Cornelius J. Jaenen, in Paul W. Bennett and Cornelius J. Jaenen, *Emerging Identities*, Toronto: Prentice-Hall, 1986, p. 7.

CHAPTER 5

FAST FORWARD

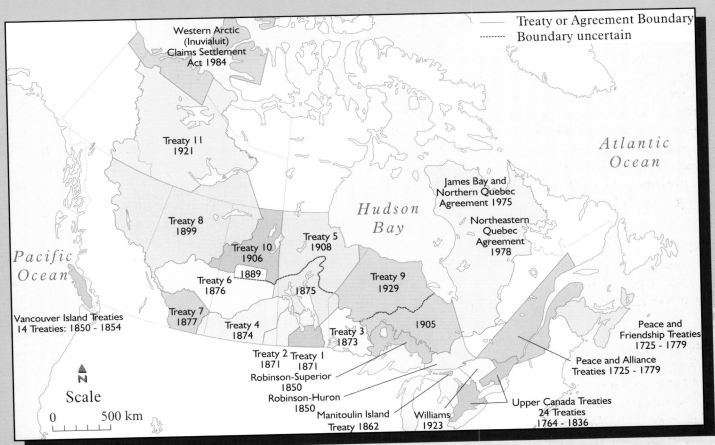

Treaty or Agreement Boundary
-------- Boundary uncertain

Western Arctic (Inuvialuit) Claims Settlement Act 1984

Treaty 11 1921

Treaty 8 1899

Pacific Ocean

Treaty 10 1906

1889

Treaty 6 1876

Treaty 5 1908

Hudson Bay

James Bay and Northern Quebec Agreement 1975

Northeastern Quebec Agreement 1978

Atlantic Ocean

Treaty 9 1929

Treaty 7 1877

Treaty 4 1874

1875

Treaty 3 1873

1905

Vancouver Island Treaties 14 Treaties: 1850 - 1854

Treaty 2 1871

Treaty 1 1871

Robinson-Superior 1850

Robinson-Huron 1850

Manitoulin Island Treaty 1862

Williams 1923

Peace and Friendship Treaties 1725 - 1779

Peace and Alliance Treaties 1725 - 1779

Upper Canada Treaties 24 Treaties 1764 - 1836

N

Scale

0   500 km

Historic treaties between First Nations and Canada cover large parts of the country. Which parts have not been covered by treaties? What do you think this could mean for the Aboriginal peoples who live there?

T he impact of European contact changed Aboriginal societies forever. As time went by, Aboriginal peoples lost more and more control over their lives. By the time Canada became a nation in 1867, they had no power in a land that was once their own.

From the Sources

In 1998, Canada acknowledged that Aboriginal peoples had not been treated fairly in the past. The government issued this Statement of Reconciliation:

Reconciliation is an ongoing process. In renewing our partnership, we must ensure that the mistakes that marked our past relationship are not repeated. The Government of Canada recognizes that policies that sought to assimilate Aboriginal people…are not the way to build a strong country. We must instead continue to find ways in which Aboriginal people can participate fully in the economic, political, cultural and social life of Canada in a manner which preserves and enhances the collective identity of Aboriginal communities.

Jane Stewart, Minister of Indian Affairs and Northern Development, January 1998

LOSING THEIR RIGHTS

Following Confederation, Canada wanted to open up the West to settlers. First, though, the government had to establish that it owned the land. The government signed a series of treaties with First Nations. The First Nations thought the treaties would help them adapt to the changes that had taken place in their world. They thought the treaties would help them preserve their culture and traditions. When they signed the treaties, they believed they were agreeing to share the land. But the government saw the treaties as a way to remove Aboriginal peoples from the land and resettle them on reserves. Then the government would own the land and it could begin to open up the West.

In 1876, the government passed the Indian Act. This gave it total control over the lives of Aboriginal peoples. The government had the power to decide who was a member of a First Nation. It had the power to decide who could receive reserve lands. It had the power to decide how much money to pay under the treaties it signed.

At the same time, the government wanted to **assimilate** Aboriginal peoples. It wanted them to give up their languages and traditions. These policies **discriminated** against Aboriginal peoples. They were denied the same rights other people in Canada had.

Things would not change for the next 100 years. Then, in the 1970s, Aboriginal peoples began to fight for their rights. They gained new confidence. They demanded that Canada honour the promises it had made to them. They would accept nothing less than being treated as equals in their homeland.

SETTLING LAND CLAIMS

Many First Nations signed treaties. But many others did not. Aboriginal leaders argued that First Nations that did not sign treaties never gave up the land. Therefore, they still held the rights to those lands. In 1973, the **Supreme Court** of Canada agreed. It said that First Nations had the right to make land claims. Since then, governments have negotiated many land agreements with First Nations.

One of the biggest land settlements involved the Nisga'a of British Columbia. In 1998, they reached a deal with the province. They agreed to give up 80 percent of their traditional lands. In return, they received:

- **self-government**
- $253 million in cash
- the rights to the forest and mineral resources in a 2,000-square-kilometre area, and
- hunting and fishing rights.

Some people felt that the Nisga'a received too much money. After all, they argued, there were only 5,000 people in the Nisga'a Nation. But the hottest issue was self-government. The Nisga'a were given widespread powers. They controlled language, culture, citizenship, taxes, health and social services, and education. The only rule was that their laws had to follow the Charter of Rights and Freedoms and the Criminal Code. Some people thought this made the Nisga'a an independent state within Canada. Most Aboriginal peoples disagreed. They viewed the Nisga'a agreement as an important victory. It created a model for future deals. Many Canadians agreed with them.

The Charter and the Code

The Canadian Charter of Rights and Freedoms was created in 1982. It guarantees that all Canadians have certain freedoms, such as the freedom to worship in their faith. It also guarantees their legal rights, such as the right to vote. The Criminal Code includes most of Canada's criminal laws.

These Nisga'a children celebrated the agreement with the Elders of their nation in August 1998 in New Aiyansh, British Columbia.

THE RICHEST CLAIM OF ALL

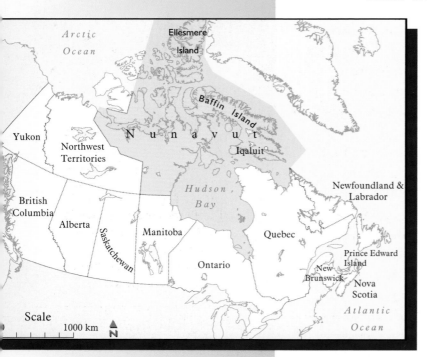

Nunavut is about the size of British Columbia, Alberta, and Yukon combined.

The largest—and richest—land settlement ever made in Canada came into effect on April 1, 1999. That's when Nunavut came into being. Its name means "Our Land" in the Inuit language of Inuktitut.

Nunavut was carved out of the eastern side of the Northwest Territories. It is 2 million square kilometres. That's about 20 percent of the country! The Inuit own 18 percent of the new territory. Their land contains many mineral deposits, including gold, silver, copper, and lead. The Inuit will be able to mine these resources and keep a share of the profits. They also received $1 billion in cash. In return, the Inuit gave up any further land claims.

About 25,000 people live in Nunavut. Eighty-five percent are Inuit. This means that Aboriginal peoples form the **majority** in the government.

The creation of Nunavut attracted attention around the world. In other countries, governments and Aboriginal peoples are discussing land claims, too. They want to see if this kind of agreement might work for them.

◀ Playback ▶

1. Do you think it was important for the government to issue the Statement of Reconciliation? Give reasons for your answer.

2. Why do you think the Supreme Court's decision in 1973 was important for Aboriginal peoples?

3. Do you think the Nisga'a agreement was fair? Give reasons for your answer.

4. (a) Do you think the creation of Nunavut is important for Aboriginal peoples across Canada? Explain your answer.
   (b) Why would the creation of Nunavut be of interest to people in other countries?

5. Do research into one other land claim settlement in Canada. Highlight the key terms of the agreement in an organizer or web.

The Debate Over Self-Government

In the early 1990s, the government did a study on Aboriginal peoples in Canada. In 1996, the study published the *Report of the Royal Commission on Aboriginal Peoples*. It recommended that a House of First Peoples be created. It would be a separate Aboriginal government. It would have the same powers as the federal and provincial governments.

This sparked debate about how such a government should be set up. The federal government wants it to be an act of Parliament. This means it would remain under federal control. The Aboriginal government would control local matters. These would include education, social services, lands, and hunting and fishing rights. But it would not have control over larger issues. These would include foreign affairs, the economy, immigration, and health care. These would remain federal powers.

Aboriginal leaders disagree. They say they have the right to govern themselves because they freely governed themselves before Europeans ever came to North America. Aboriginal leaders don't want self-government to be an act of Parliament, either. They say this would give Parliament the power to change their government if it wanted to. They would not have to ask Aboriginal peoples how they felt about it. Aboriginal peoples want self-government to be written into the Constitution. This would guarantee their rights.

Toward a Better Future

Today, Aboriginal leaders and governments are trying to open up communications. They are working to correct the mistakes of the past. They are trying to improve the lives of Aboriginal peoples. They are hoping to create a fairer society. Both sides want Canada to be a place where Aboriginal peoples are recognized, valued, and respected.

The Rights of the People

Today, the rights of all Canadians are guaranteed by the Constitution. This document can only be changed if the federal and provincial governments agree following a complex **amending formula**. So if Aboriginal self-government is written into the Constitution, it would be very difficult to change it.

Aboriginal Peoples in Canada Today

The government surveyed all Canadians in 2001. It showed that:
- Over 1.3 million people in Canada said they have some Aboriginal **ancestry**. That is 4.4 percent of the population. This is up from 3.8 percent in 1996. Over 957,000 people said they were a member of a First Nation. Over 266,000 people said they were Métis. Over 51,000 people said they were Inuit. Over 44,000 people said they had more than one Aboriginal origin.

- Ontario has the most Aboriginal people. But they make up less than 2 percent of the population. In Nunavut, Aboriginal peoples make up 85 percent of the population.
- Almost half—49 percent—of all Aboriginal peoples live in urban areas; 31 percent live on reserves; 19.5 percent live in rural areas.
- Winnipeg has the highest number of Aboriginal people. It is followed by Edmonton, Vancouver, Calgary, Toronto, Saskatoon, Regina, Ottawa-Gatineau, Montreal, and Victoria.

Based on the 2001 Census of Canada, Statistics Canada

Aboriginal Population by Group, 2001

	First Nations	Métis	Inuit
Canada	**608,850**	**292,305**	**45,070**
Newfoundland and Labrador	7,040	5,480	4,560
Prince Edward Island	1,035	220	20
Nova Scotia	12,920	3,135	350
New Brunswick	11,495	4,290	155
Quebec	51,125	15,855	9,530
Ontario	131,560	48,340	1,375
Manitoba	90,340	56,800	340
Saskatchewan	83,745	43,695	235
Alberta	84,995	66,060	1,090
British Columbia	118,295	44,265	800
Yukon	5,600	535	140
Northwest Territories	10,615	3,580	3,910
Nunavut	95	55	22,560

2001 Census of Canada, Statistics Canada

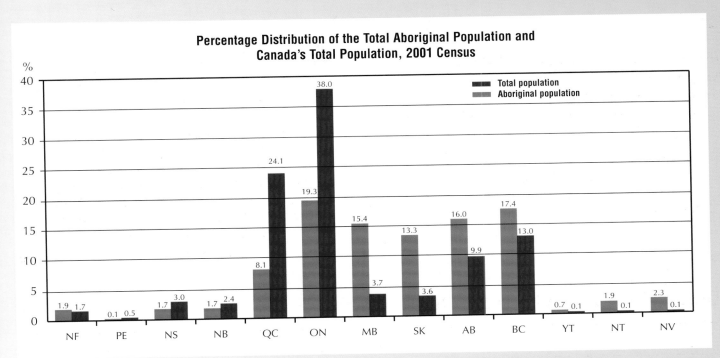

Percentage Distribution of the Total Aboriginal Population and Canada's Total Population, 2001 Census

2001 Census of Canada, Statistics Canada

Look at the table of Aboriginal population on page 62.

1. Which province or territory has:

   (a) the most First Nations?

   (b) the most Métis?

   (c) the most Inuit?

2. (a) Which three provinces and/or territories have the most Aboriginal peoples?

   (b) Which three provinces and/or territories have the fewest Aboriginal peoples?

3. What is the total number of Aboriginal people in your province or territory?

   Now look at the graph. It shows the percentage distribution of the total Aboriginal population and Canada's total population.

4. Why do you think the percentage of Aboriginal people living in the West and the North is higher than the total population in these regions? Think about what you have learned in this book.

◄ Playback ►

1. (a) Divide the class into two groups. One group should represent Aboriginal leaders. The other should represent the Canadian government. Each group should outline its position on self-government. Then hold a round-table discussion to express the two points of view.
   (b) How do you think the government and Aboriginal leaders might reach a common agreement about self-government?

2. The federal government has created National Aboriginal Day. It was established so Canadians could celebrate the heritage, culture, and contributions of Aboriginal peoples in Canada. Find out more about this special day. Then create a poster to promote National Aboriginal Day.

The Back Story

Historical evidence helps us understand the past. It can answer the questions how, why, when, and where an event happened and who was involved. In the past, people who study history have thought of historical evidence only as written documents and artifacts.

Aboriginal peoples did not write their histories down, though. Their histories are told through the oral stories they pass down from one generation to another. The Nisga'a wanted to use these stories to prove their land claims. A judge in British Columbia said no. He ruled that the stories were not reliable since no one could prove they were true.

The Nisga'a appealed the judge's decision. They took their case to the Supreme Court of Canada. In 1997, the Supreme Court agreed with the Nisga'a. They said that oral histories were valid. The Nisga'a were allowed to present their stories and songs as evidence that they had always lived on their land.

The Goal

With a partner, write an argument out-lining the reasons why the oral histories of Aboriginal peoples are valid evidence of their past.

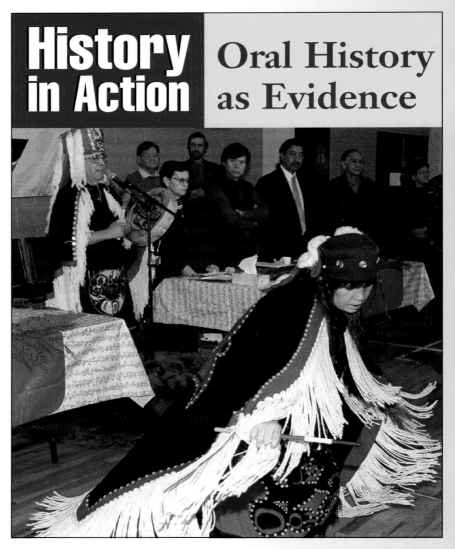

History in Action   Oral History as Evidence

Aboriginal peoples celebrated the Supreme Court's decision on oral histories in 1997.

The Steps

1. Do research to find out more about the oral tradition.
2. Refer to the Charter of Rights and Freedoms. Find any points that support your case.
3. Brainstorm possible arguments for your case with a partner. Jot down all your ideas.
4. Prepare an outline of your presentation. Begin with an introduction that clearly states your purpose. Then, prepare a list of ideas and facts that support your point of view. Be sure to arrange your ideas in order. End your presentation by summarizing your arguments.
5. You may want to develop your outline into an oral presentation and deliver it in a mock session of the Supreme Court of Canada.

Evaluating Your Work

These are the criteria you should think about as you complete your work. Your work should:
  • have a powerful opening
  • be well organized, with clear and logical arguments
  • have a powerful conclusion
  • be an effective oral presentation

Glossary

absolute monarch a king or queen who has unlimited power

alliance a friendly agreement between groups

amending formula a method for making changes to the Constitution

ancestry a person's parents, grandparents, and other ancestors

artifact an object made by human activity

assassinate to murder a ruler or well-known person

assimilate to make a minority group of people practice the customs of a larger group

baptize to sprinkle someone with water in a religious ceremony

beatify to declare a dead person to be blessed in heaven

bias to favour one side over another

burial rites a ceremony for burying a dead person

cartographer a person who makes maps

contact the first interaction between Aboriginal peoples and Europeans

democratic a government that is chosen by the people

dialect the form of a language used by a particular group

discriminate to treat a person differently because of race, gender, age, or religion

epidemic a disease that spreads rapidly throughout a society

filles du roi "the king's daughters"—young French women who came to New France to marry

immunity the ability to resist a disease

majority the greater number

migrate to move from one place to another

missionary a person sent by the Church to spread religion

mystic a person who possesses ancient religious powers

navigational for use in charting and controlling a ship's route

potlatch a celebration in which gifts are given

primary source first-hand evidence made at or near the time an event took place

self-government government of a group by its own people

semi-nomadic to occasionally move from one place to another

shaman an Aboriginal spiritual leader and healer

social equality where all people in a society are equal to one another

staple a raw material such as fish, wheat, or timber

subsistence a means of staying alive by using only those things that are needed

Supreme Court the highest court in Canada

treason the act of betraying one's nation

treaty a legal agreement between nations

truce an agreement to stop fighting for a period of time

umiak a large, flat-bottomed boat used by the Inuit

world view a group's view of the world and its relationship to it

Index

A
Aboriginals, 1-4, 57, 62-63
    creation stories, 8-9
    cultural areas, 16
    government, 12, 13
    and land treaties, 14, 57, 58
    languages, 10
    names, 1
    population, 62, 63
    and self-government, 61
    societies, 7, 15
    spiritual beliefs, 11, 14, 46,
    47, 48
    and trade, 15, 37, 43
    alcohol, 42
Algonquin, 27, 38, 40, 41, 47
Arctic, 36

B
Basques, 34, 38
Beothuk, 32-33
black robes, 53
Bourgeoys, Marguérite, 50
Brébeuf, Jean de, 49
Brûlé, Étienne, 39

C
Cabot, John, 17, 19
Canada: A People's History, 5,
    12, 22, 32, 51
Cartier, Jacques, 20-22, 37
Catholic Church, 45-46, 47
Champlain, Samuel de, 4, 24-27,
    38, 40, 47
Charter of Rights and Freedoms,
    59
codfish, 30-31
Columbus, Christopher, 18-19
Constitution, 61
contact, first, 5, 6, 15
coureurs de bois, 38, 42
creation stories, 8-9

D
Dekanawideh, 12
diseases, 6, 21, 33, 41
Dominican Republic, 19
Donnacona, 20-22
Duval, Jean, 38

E
Europe, 4, 12, 18, 19, 30, 34
Europeans, 5, 6, 32, 36, 37
explorers, 17-22

F
First Nations see Aboriginals
fish, 19
    see also codfish
fishing, wet and dry methods, 31
fur trade, 20, 33, 37-38, 41, 42-43

H
Haiti, 19
historical evidence, 64
l'Hôtel-Dieu, 50
House of First Peoples, 61
Huron Carol, 49
Huron Nation, 27, 38, 39, 40, 41
    Jesuit influence, 47-49, 53-55

I
l'Incarnation, Marie de, 51
Indian Act, 58
Inuit, 36, 60
Iroquois, 20, 22, 26, 27, 41
    raids against, 40-41
Iroquois Confederacy, 13

J
Jesuits, 47-48, 49, 53, 54

K
Kanawaké Reserve, 52

L
Lalemant, Father Charles, 56
land claims, 58-60
land treaties, 14, 57, 58
languages, 10
longhouse, 13

M
Mance, Jeanne, 50
medicines, 21
Mi'kmaq Nation, 6, 20, 37
missionaries, 6, 41, 42, 46-48
Montagnais, 38, 40, 41
Monts, Pierre de, 24, 26

N
New France, 39, 41
    and Catholic Church, 46-47,
    50-51
    and fur trade, 20, 26-27, 38
Newfoundland, 32, 33
Nisga'a, 59, 64
Nunavut, 60
nuns, 50-51

O
oral stories, 5, 10, 64
Order of Good Cheer, 25

P
plankton, 30
population surveys, 62-63
Port Royal, 26, 27
potlatches, 14
primary sources, 56
Protestant Reformation, 45

Q
Quebec, 26, 27, 38

R
Récollets, 47
religion, 11, 45-46

S
Sainte-Marie-among-the-Hurons,
    54, 55
scurvy, 21, 24
self-government, 61
settlers, 32
shamans, 11
Shawnadithit, 32, 33
spiritual beliefs, 11, 14, 46, 47, 48
St. Lawrence River, 21, 23, 24,
    26, 38, 42
Stadacona, 21-22, 26
Statement of Reconciliation, 58
Ste. Croix, 24
stories, 5
    creation, 8-9
    oral, 10, 64

T
Tadoussac, 38
Tekakwitha, Kateri, 52
timeline, 2-5
trade, 15, 29
    see also fur trade
treaties see land treaties

V
visual evidence, 44
voyageurs, 42-43

W
whaling, 34-36
women, 13, 50-52
world views, 1, 46

Photo Credits

Cover top: J.D. Kelly / Rogers Communications, left, CBC, *Canada: A People's History*, right, *France Bringing the Faith to the Indians of New France*, attributed to Claude Francois dit Frère Luc. Collection du monastère des Ursulines de Québec. Copyright: Musée national des beaux-arts du Québec, Patrick Altman; Page 1: map, Paperglyphs; Page 2: top: J.D. Kelly / Rogers Communications, bottom: National Archives of Canada, C-0011201; Page 3: National Archives of Canada, C-011201; Page 4: The Granger Collection, 0007681; Page 5: top: Chuck Stoody / CP Photo Archive, bottom: CBC, *Canada: A People's History*; Page 6: National Archives of Canada, C-000810; Page 7: National Archives of Canada, C-001994; Page 8: *Birth of the Earth* by Arnold Jacobs / Two Turtle Studio; Page 9: Geographical Visual Aids; Page 10: map, Paperglyphs; Page 11: *Medicine Pipe Stem Dance*, by Paul Kane, Stark Museum of Art, 31.78/148. Stark Museum of Art, Orange, Texas; Page 12: left: Superstock 1158/21041/1/P30G, right: CBC, *Canada: A People's History* (12); Page 13: National Archives of Canada, C-09767; Page 14: *The Tyee Potlatch* by James Gerrais, British Columbia Archives, PDP00714; Page 15: map, Paperglyphs; Page 16: map, Paperglyphs; Page 17: J.D. Kelly / Rogers Communications; Page 18: Mary Evans Picture Library 10015574a; Page 19: map, Paperglyphs; Page 20: National Archives of Canada, C-011226; Page 21: National Archives of Canada, C-013938; Page 22: left: CBC, *Canada: A People's History*, right: National Archives of Canada, C-012235; Page 23: map, Paperglyphs; Page 24: National Archives of Canada, C-147846; Page 25: *Scene in the Mess of the Second Quebec Settlement, 1627* by Francis Back, Canadian Museum of Civilization, S94-13, 215; Page 26: top: Stewart Museum at the Fort, Ile Sainte-Hélène, Montreal, bottom: map, Paperglyphs; Page 27: National Archives of Canada, C-09711; Page 28: J.D. Kelly / Rogers Communications; Page 29: National Archives of Canada, C-103059; Page 30: map, Paperglyphs; Page 31 top: National Archives of Canada, NMC-1867, bottom: National Archives of Canada, C-0033686; Page 32: CBC, *Canada: A People's History*; Page 33: National Archives of Canada, C-028544; Page 34: Canadian Museum of Civilization; Page 35: National Archives of Canada, C-032706; Page 36: Canadian Museum of Civilization; Page 37: National Archives of Canada, C-114485; Page 38: The Granger Collection, 0008580; Page 39: Rogers Communications; Page 40: Musée du Château Ramezay; Page 42: top: *Le Massacre des Hurons par les Iroquois* by Joseph Légaré. Musée national des beaux-arts du Québec, 57.204, bottom: National Archives of Canada, C-002771; Page 45: *France Bringing the Faith to the Indians of New France*, attributed to Claude Francois dit Frère Luc. Collection du monastère des Ursulines de Québec. Copyright: Musée national des beaux-arts du Québec, Patrick Altman; Page 47: map, Paperglyphs; Page 48: National Archives of Canada, C-005855; Page 50: top: Archives Religieuses Hospitalières de Saint-Joseph, bottom: Marguerite Bourgeoys at the first school of Ville-Marie by Sister Saint-René Lachance, C.N.D. Musée Marguerite-Bourgeoys; Page 51: CBC, *Canada: A People's History*; Page 52: Courtesy of Norm Léveillée; Page 53: National Archives of Canada, C-005855; Page 54: Courtesy of Sainte-Marie-among-the-Hurons; Page 55: Canadian Heritage Gallery; Page 56: © CORBIS / BETTMAN / MAGMA; Page 57: map, Paperglyphs; Page 59: Nick Procaylo / CP Photo Archives; Page 60: map, Paperglyphs; Page 63: Percentage distribution of the total Aboriginal identity population and Canada's total population, 2001 Census from the Statistics Canada website, http://www12.statcan.ca/english/ census01/teacher's kit/activity11_part2_chart.cfm; Page 64: Chick Stoody / CP Photo Archives.

Reviewers

Kathryn Brownell, Terry Fox School, Toronto, Ontario

Manny Calisto, West St. Paul School, West St. Paul, Manitoba

Greer Coe, Montague Intermediate School, Montague, Prince Edward Island

Rick Elliott, John Buchan School, Toronto, Ontario

Sheri Epstein, Langstaff High School, Thornhill, Ontario

Christine Greene, Avalon East School Board, St. John's, Newfoundland

Joanne Wheeler, St. Margaret School, Calgary, Alberta